DEDICATION

Capital Letters is dedicated to my friend Brenda Henderson, who made the visits to London such fun by sending supportive, amusing texts and sharing many of the adventures.

ACKNOWLEDGEMENTS

Elizabeth Training, for the opportunity to travel frequently to London, without which *Capital Letters* could not have been written.
Bren, Ruth, and the many friends and family members, for their support and encouragement through each stage of writing.
Helen Thompson, for sharing your own experiences of London.
Marg and Dave, for the day's outing to the Ffestiniog steam railway.
Anna, my god-daughter, for inspiration and ideas for the book cover.

PREFACE

At the beginning of 2006, I was given a contract to assess managers within the care industry in London for the NVQ in Care.

I had previously assessed a range of NVQ courses in Health and Social Care locally. The proposition of working in London was therefore both exciting but also slightly daunting because it involved meeting new people in different care settings and visiting different parts of London, which were new to me, and travelling up to and across the city by public transport. It soon became apparent that neither the train journey to the capital nor the navigation once there was to be straightforward. Many of the situations were very funny, some frustrating and some almost unbelievable.

I always carried my laptop and my mobile phone as well as a street map of London. All these essential accessories were intended to protect against getting lost. In addition to keeping in contact with friends, students and colleagues, my laptop also enabled me to work on the train and at the care locations.

On each visit I set off in my car from my home in a small village in West Sussex to catch the train at Shoreham-by-Sea. My intended destination each time was London Victoria, and on arrival there I often stopped off at Bonapartes to take stock and have a much-needed cup of coffee and croissant.

I am not sure at what point I decided to start writing letters to my friend 'B' in Southampton, but it quickly became a habit as I met interesting people and experienced events which were often not of my making.

The early letters show the frustration and lack of time management in preparation for the forthcoming day, which involved not only organising myself but also two chocolate Labrador puppies (Max and Bruno) who needed to be walked and fed.

In time I became an old hand at commuting, and the later letters reflect this more laid-back approach to both travelling and the work involved. This would not have been possible without the support of my long-suffering friend and companion 'BJ', with whom I have shared a house for over 30 years.

Inevitably, travelling to London evoked memories of previous visits and journeys, and accounts of these are included in some of the letters.

It soon became apparent that my knowledge of London's famous places and people was sadly lacking, and I consequently began to research ones which I passed through en route to my student destinations or visited on previous occasions.

The letters have proved to be fun to write and share with someone who knows me well and is a dear friend. I have recounted the adventures to other friends who have supported and encouraged me to publish the adventures in London which have become Capital Letters. I hope you, the reader, enjoy them too and perhaps can identify with some of the experiences and types of interesting people encountered on these and other train journeys.

Dear B

What a day! A London adventure! This is my first visit to assess a manager of a care home as part of my new contract and working for myself as self-employed.

I woke up to the squeaking of Bruno at 5.55 a.m.; I really must put a sleeping draught in his water. I felt very tired, like someone had stolen some hours out of the night (but the clocks haven't been put forward yet).

I staggered into the kitchen with the intention of walking the dogs before heading to Town, but in the end I didn't have time and BJ did it.

I managed to find time to shower, dress and have a bowl of cereal, but no time to put on make-up. BJ offered me her new briefcase for my laptop which fits better into it and which is too big for her laptop. That was a kind thought, but I managed to break the zip by stuffing too much into it! S***! After struggling with it for a few minutes I fixed it sufficiently to contain the laptop so it was at least functional.

Then I couldn't find the address of where to go; or my diary; or any change for the car park at the station! More blue air, in fact navy blue air (BJ should be beatified now!). It's amazing how our friendship has stood the test of time through the ups and downs of life over the past 30 years. BJ just takes my frustrations in her stride and carries on calmly preparing for her own day's work.

Too late I realised that the trouser suit I had put on was too loose at the waist, and nearly falling down (I have lost weight since Christmas, probably due to all the recent dog walking). I spent half the day hitching them up and trying not to trip over my own feet!

I arrived at the station still half asleep with two minutes to spare; I had to risk the ticket machine on the platform. Fortunately, it worked quickly and gave me a ticket and my credit card back without eating it.

Boarding the train to Victoria, I realised I hadn't put on any earrings and felt half dressed. The train was crowded with people who looked just as dozy as I felt.

I tried to do the Su Doku but couldn't, so I gave up and sulked all the way to London.

I thought about the first time I travelled to London when I was 15 years old, and the excitement of that occasion. I will tell you about it sometime.

We arrived at Victoria and I decided that I needed to pause for thought, buy a coffee and get a grip on the day's visit!

As I went through the ticket barrier, the machine unexpectedly ate my ticket and I realised I hadn't got an underground ticket at Shoreham and would have to queue for ages to buy one! Another complication! More delay!

I felt an even greater need to indulge in a cappuccino and an apple croissant (comfort eating, I think). In the nearest café I bought these two items and I was hoping to get 20p in change so I could go to the loo on the station. But there were no 20p's in the change.

Dilemma!

Looking round, I was cheered up by the sight of a loo in the café and it was free. I made my way towards it and the door was shut fast! To get in you have to ask the staff for the code to the key pad. How embarrassing is that? I sidled up to a waitress and asked for the code; she said, "2020." "2020?" (I blinked, thinking that my vision cannot have improved that much since my last visit to the optician.) However, I then climbed some stairs to the loo and wondered why it needed to be kept locked because it was really seedy with no soap! I powdered my nose and put on some lippy and began to feel half human, but I was still missing my earrings.

Down on the station concourse again, I decided to be very extravagant and buy a pair of earrings at the Swatch shop. I looked carefully at the selection and found the cheapest pair. They were silver rectangles and quite small. I thought they looked OK when I held them up by my ear lobes, and I decided to buy them. The price of vanity was £17, but I felt more cheerful and confident!

I then waited in a queue for 20 minutes to buy an Oyster card, thinking this was a smart move and I needn't be bothered with underground or bus tickets for a while (it costs £30).

Entering the underground, I decided it would be quicker to go via the Victoria line to Kings Cross and change to the Hammersmith line to travel to Ladbroke Grove. On the tube I was further cheered by a silly rhyme by Edward Lear:

> There was an old man from Blackheath,
>
> Whose head was adorned with a wreath,
>
> Of oysters and spice, pickled onions and mice
>
> That uncommon old man of Blackheath.

I have *The Complete Nonsense of Edward Lear* on my bookshelf at home. I must look this limerick up to see if it has a title and read some of his other stories and poems. I've had the book for years and can't remember who gave it to me. Probably someone else with a way-out sense of humour!

I must have a go at limericks sometime; I reckon I could write some just as silly!

I changed at Kings Cross, according to plan, and boarded the Hammersmith train (I knew this was the right one because it said so on the front of the train and on the platform gantry). As we left Baker Street, however, an announcement came over the tannoy: "This train will now go to Parsons Green!" WOT?! Why? Where's that? There was no forthcoming explanation or justification for the change in destination and it's definitely not on the way to Hammersmith! Several other folks looked a bit anxious as well, also wondering whether they were hearing things. But no, the same message was repeated: "This is now a District line train going to Parson's Green!" "I do not believe it!" I said aloud in true Victor Meldrew fashion. But it's true, so I got off at the next stop, Edgware Road, to catch a Hammersmith train again; the next train is not due for seven minutes. Seven minutes! I was already late and it was still six stops away; at that rate I would not get there until lunchtime. I thought to myself, it's quicker to go to Madeira!

So I decided to get a taxi and exited the underground, to stand in the middle of the road waving my arms frantically, trying to hail a passing cab. Fortunately one stopped; the driver probably had no other option except to run me over. The cabbie knew the name of the road but was not sure where the care home was situated, yet assured me he would find it. I told him my woes and he listened sympathetically, as we cruised up and down St Mark's Road looking for it. Both of us cheered to see the sign of the care home at last at the far end. I arrived at my destination and felt much better for my encounter with this friendly taxi driver.

Today I was visiting a block of flats for people with moderate to severe learning difficulties. The entrance to the home was not on the main street, as I expected, but through an archway to one side. I rang the doorbell and was greeted by a chap (20–30ish) who was holding a toilet roll in his hand.

Is this some kind of new handshake or a hygiene precaution which has been introduced that I don't know about? I asked myself, because you never know in cosmopolitan London and it's impossible to keep up to date with the ever increasing health and safety procedures. Anyway, I must have raised my eyebrows or something because he hastily explained that he has a cold. (Guess I must make more effort to control my facial expressions in future!) So it's OK, I haven't missed anything.

If you think about it loo rolls are probably more convenient when you're working, and it was probably a perk from work anyway!

I enjoyed my visit and the manager had completed several pieces of work, which made my life a whole lot easier. I definitely warmed to this chap! Especially when I worked through lunch and he bought me a ham sandwich with too much mayonnaise, but I didn't complain and washed it down with a cup of coffee. I left at around 2.15 and decided to catch a bus back to Victoria.

At first I couldn't find the bus stop because of all the roadworks. Undeterred I walked round the corner, and there it was and a No. 52 bus just pulling in alongside!

At last I am homeward bound and ascended to the top deck, which is easier said than done because of the way the bus hurtles along bus lanes. I like to sit on the top deck, preferably at the front, to see the sights, but today someone has vomited and there is the most unpleasant smell so I moved much further back!

I was further cheered by swapping funny messages with your good self even though you had difficulty understanding my unique tec speak.

All in all it has been an adventure and the day definitely ended on a better note than it started.

Glad you were part of it, B; thought you might like to hear about it.

Love, M

PS. Just thought of a couple of limericks. What do you think?

Limerick 1

There was a young man in Hyde Park,

Who thought it fun in the dark

To jump out from a shrub and grab someone's grub,

And then run off for a lark.

Limerick 2

A young lass who lived by the docks

Cut off her fair flowing locks.

Her mother was cross at this terrible loss,

Crying, "See how everyone mocks."

Oh well, I tried!

M

PPS. Enjoy your weekend and the concert at the Royal Albert Hall; I've been there on a couple of occasions and have found out more about it. There is such a lot of information on the Royal Albert Hall, B, but I think you will enjoy reading it; it's certainly an inspiring place with an exciting history.

The Royal Albert Hall

The project for building the Royal Albert Hall started following the success of the Great Exhibition in nearby Hyde Park in 1851, which had been supported by Prince Albert. The Exhibition celebrated many innovations from industry and artists from around the world. This was an attempt to bring together the best of technology and creativity to improve people's lifestyles. The profits from the Great Exhibition were used to partly fund the building of the great hall; part of the vision of Prince Albert for an estate for cultural, scientific and academic institutions to be all together on one site. Sadly, he died of typhoid fever before its completion. The name was changed to the Royal Albert Hall in 1867 when Queen Victoria laid the foundation stone.

The Hall finally opened in 1871. The inspiration for the design came from Henry Cole, who had worked closely with Prince Albert on the project. Henry Cole visited Europe and came back with the idea of a Roman amphitheatre and designed the elliptical shape with its central arena, which was approved by Queen Victoria. Her only comment on seeing it during construction was that it 'looks like the British Constitution', and other folks apparently thought that it looked like a giant wedding cake!

Originally the Hall was intended to be much larger to accommodate 30,000 people, but this was beyond the available resources, and the more modest building seating 7,000 was opened in 1871 with the music of the

Grenadier Guards and the smell of Eau de Cologne pumped through the ventilation system!

To raise money for the Hall (projected cost £200,000; which came in below budget at £199,748!), seats were sold for £100 each with a 999-year lease attached.

A royal charter signed by Queen Victoria (1867) still governs the Hall today, and she attended the first concert held there on 8th May 1867.

There were problems with the acoustics in the Hall from the beginning, so a giant awning was hung beneath the dome to correct the reverberations, echoes and blind spots. Of course it collected dust! But it wasn't until 1949 that it was cleaned, using eight giant vacuum cleaners. It took a day and a half to clear it up (over 100 tons of it). I'm glad the awning was strong and I wonder where they put all that dust. I bet there were a few sneezing fits without the rigid health and safety rules which would be in force today. In 1960 the acoustics were improved with the erection of fibreglass diffusers in the roof.

It was here that The Wine Society started, following an exhibition of food and drink in 1874. A large quantity of Portuguese wine was left over in the cellars, so a series of dinner parties was organised to consume it!

The centenary of the Hall was celebrated with a complete cleaning and refurbishment programme both inside and out. Further improvements have been added, including a new organ, new stalls and the reconstruction of the South Porch, opened by Her Majesty The Queen in 2004.

Great piano and orchestra performances have taken place here as well as ballet, balls, exhibitions and trade fairs. In the first half of the twentieth century, sport and the first cinema were featured, together with motor shows, tennis and comedy. The Hall was closed during part of the Second World War. The BBC proms were held here for the first time in 1941.

The names of celebrities from many countries who have been part of the events and contributed to the success of the Hall is endless, and makes it arguably one of the most exciting venues in London, if not the world.

M

LETTER 2.

7th March 2006

Dear B

I promised to tell you about the first time I visited London. Well, here goes.

It was in 1962 and the Diamond Jubilee of the Girls' Brigade (then The Girls' Life Brigade – I never did understand why the name was changed and the 'Life' knocked out of the organisation). I'd never travelled much beyond my small hometown in Somerset until then, so this trip was very exciting! We stayed in Kent with friends of the captain and then travelled into London for the 'Great Day'. There was to be a rally in the Royal Albert Hall, but only officers and a few selected girls were going to attend because of space, I guess. It didn't matter – I was going to London! We were going to Buckingham Palace to see the changing of the guards. We were to walk in Hyde Park and visit Westminster Abbey. All places which I had learned about in school (or GLB) and only seen in picture books. At home we did not have a TV and I had only seen the Queen once on television. I can just remember it as one of my earliest memories. We lived next door to the Baptist church, and one of its members hired a television for the occasion of the Coronation.

Anyway, on this day we marched down the Mall, hundreds of us all in our navy uniforms (including hats) behind the bands. I always loved marching on church parades and carrying the flag in its leather holster. Our uniforms were made of navy blue serge. We wore red and blue ties held in place with the badge of GLB and white gloves plus stockings with seams (held up by suspenders, of course!). I can't remember what the criteria were for promotion through the ranks; I had one white chevron on the right sleeve (I think I was a lance corporal). The left sleeve displayed an array of circular cloth badges showing the achievements in a range of skills from wiring a plug to country dancing. I felt very proud marching along and hoped that I wouldn't get out of step – that would have been awful.

There was always a series of military-style commands to get us into formation: 'Single rank size!' which meant that I was always at the end of the line because I was so short. The command: 'Odd numbers forward and even numbers stepping back' in some way rearranged the line, and eventually I ended up somehow in the middle and hidden from view. Finally off we went with the command: 'By the left, quick march!'

I have a photograph of me standing outside the gates of the Palace dressed in uniform, mouth wide open in amazement, looking rather like a goldfish. It's amazing to think that we are able to go inside Buckingham Palace now that it's open to the public during the summer months.

After the march down the Mall we visited Westminster Abbey, a church with a 1,000-year history originally built in the reign of Edward the Confessor with various additions through the centuries. I was especially interested in the North West Tower, which houses ten bells and a one-handed clock.

The coronations of monarchs have been conducted here. The first was William the Conqueror (1066) on Christmas Day! I was impressed by the grandeur of the coronation chair constructed by Edward I in 1301. We were also shown the tomb of the Unknown Soldier who was killed in the First World War.

Poet's Corner was also pointed out, where Geoffrey Chaucer was buried in 1400. About 3,000 people in total are buried in the Abbey, including nine monarchs, and we spent some time reading the inscriptions on the tombs and monuments.

I have been back to Westminster Abbey on several occasions since my first visit and always admire the Gothic architecture and beautiful stained glass windows. There is always stillness here and I invariably pause to sit quietly for a while and be at peace.

This first time in London is unforgettable and I think fired my passion for the capital. Certainly I was more excited then than I am today! Guess everyone else took the responsibility then and knew their way around!

So much for musing on early memories...

Hope to hear your story sometime about your first visit to the capital.

Love, M

LETTER 3.

14th March 2006

Dear B

I have been working in London again today.

There were no problems of importance except that one of the computers at the ticket window was down and I had to wait a little but it didn't matter, I had lots of time before the train was due.

No parking problems either; no rush today. I have been up since 6 a.m. and walked the dogs; they still have a mind of their own when out for a walk but usually come quickly if I put my hand in my pocket for a biscuit. The way to a dog's heart is certainly through its stomach; although I thought that only applied to men! I am glad BJ is back safely from her trip to New Zealand and will be able to walk them in the mornings again.

On the train today, which was quite crowded, there was a blind man with his golden Labrador retriever. He was standing on the platform with no other companion than his dog. I thought how courageous he was to travel alone.

There was also a group of young French students, about nine or ten years of age, I guess. I only knew they were French because I could catch the odd word or phrase as they chatted noisily to each other. They spoke too quickly for me to get the gist of their conversation, and my vocabulary is very limited anyway. They all got off at Hove, which was a relief.

I couldn't imagine what was on in London on a grey day like today – not quite the day for walking in Hyde Park as we did last year when it was so sunny and bright.

Remember how much we enjoyed that Saturday morning? We walked to Hyde Park from the hotel and the sun was shining and it was quite mild for February. We were treated to the spectacle of the Household Cavalry on horseback, returning to their barracks from Buckingham Palace after the changing of the guards had taken place a little earlier. They looked so grand in their helmets, highly polished boots and immaculately neat uniforms. I love their black horses; so well groomed and their coats always shine.

There were also cyclists and people jogging, all enjoying the park, and walkers strolling like ourselves in no hurry to get anywhere but just take in the sight of the spring flowers and early flowering shrubs and listen to the sounds of cooing pigeons and passing traffic in the distance.

There were Canada geese stretching their wings on the lawn and ducks arrayed in their mating finery; the bright-green heads of the drakes and the polished brown of the females with blue and white flashes on their wings.

We visited the fountain built as a memorial to Princess Diana. It seems only a short time since she died in that awful car crash in France, but I think it was 1997.

I have read more about the memorial since our visit and discovered that the fountain was designed by a United States architect, Kathryn Gustafson, and cost £3.6m. Its shape is based on an oval stone ring.

We walked by the side of the fountain where the water was bubbling down a gentle slope. Further on we could see the other stream tumbling and cascading along. Then we came to the tranquil pool where the two streams meet. Kathryn Gustafson apparently said the contrasting halves would reflect the different parts of the Princess's life, not only the joyous times but also the turmoil she experienced. I think she succeeded in achieving this effect, don't you?

I also found a quote from the BBC news, at the time of the fountain's commission, by Kathryn Gustafson. She said, "The concept is based upon the qualities of the Princess that were the most loved and cherished... inclusiveness and accessibility." I think the architect has achieved that too.

The train stopped at East Croydon, and there was another interesting guy who took a seat beside me on the train. He had two crutches and was hopping along and balancing on one leg somewhat precariously! Then I noticed he had no option because he only had one leg anyway. That's courageous too, especially if you don't get a seat before the train starts off again. He eventually got off at Clapham Junction, and again I admired his agility and balancing act when combating the narrow corridor and step down to the platform.

I thought about my mum and her difficulty travelling by train with an artificial leg and having to hold on firmly when negotiating the steep step up into the train, especially where there were gaps between the carriage and platform edge.

Today, I was visiting a Catholic nursing home in Kensington and Chelsea where I had not been before so it was an adventure finding my way there. I have prepared for the journey across London and have topped up my Oyster card and knew it should be only two stops on the tube and quicker than the bus.

We seemed to arrive at Victoria quickly today!

There was no time for coffee and croissants at Bonapartes because I wanted to allow plenty of time to find the new place and was not sure how much foot slogging would be involved, walking from the underground to the home.

In my haste to get to my destination I boarded the tube train on the Victoria line instead of the Circle or District. I was daydreaming, I think, and just following the crowd. Hey ho! I thought the day was going a bit too smoothly! I got off at Green Park, crossed the platform, retraced my steps to Victoria and found the Circle/District line.

Eventually, arriving at Gloucester Road tube station, I had to locate my position on my street map. It's funny how my destinations manage always to be half off the page or in the fold. No exception today! Fortunately, I found the place without too much effort and realised I had been there once before on a one-off visit to another student last year.

I rang the door bell and the door opened automatically; I was greeted in the foyer by the receptionist and I explained the reason for my visit and asked to see my two students. "They are in Mass," she said and fetched another carer, who I recognised from my last visit. She invited me to go to Mass, which was just starting, and set off quickly through the building before I had time to argue. I had no option but to follow, and after wandering through endless corridors, so that I was totally lost, we arrived at the chapel. She took my coat, briefcase and handbag (which had my mobile phone, train ticket, purse, etc. in it, so that I felt like I may never get out again). I began to understand how prisoners must feel when arrested and have all personal belongings taken away or have passports confiscated! I was totally unprepared for this! What are you up to now, God, I wonder? (Maybe because I have been out of sorts and didn't go to church on Sunday He thinks He will catch me unawares on Friday!)

I was ushered in quickly to the back of the little chapel. It felt rather like a foreign country, especially when the 'nun' (I thought they were nuns even though they didn't wear habits) was speaking with a strong accent about the music. I decided she was probably Italian because of the Catholic link with Rome. Later I discovered that it's a Spanish accent and most of them are Spanish. So much for my knowledge of European accents!

The service was interesting – I had never been to a Catholic Mass before but it was quite like the high Anglican. Looking around, I saw some residents, some visitors and some carers although it was quite difficult to decide who was what entirely. The order of service proved difficult to follow so I gave up and just followed what the rest of the congregation was doing; standing, sitting, kneeling, hoping I was getting it right. It was an enjoyable experience although it went on for about one and a half hours! There was one song that I knew so of course I sang it lustily!

At the end of the normal Eucharist there was a reading for each of the 14 Stations of the Cross because it is Lent. It was quite moving; the obvious humility and sincerity of the participants was awe-inspiring.

I still had no idea which of the people present were my students and started trying to guess, but it was impossible so I gave up. At the end I was relieved to have my belongings restored to me. Phew – I hadn't been captured and interned after all! The two students fortunately recognised me and introduced themselves.

I enjoyed talking and working with the two students for the rest of the day, both of whom are Spanish and have worked for years in Ghana. I think there is unrest there so they have been sent home. There was so much light in both their eyes, I knew they had great faith.

They were very hospitable and brought me real coffee and fruit even though I had my own sandwich.

A thought-provoking day!

Love, M

LETTER 4.

1st April 2006

Dear B

Spring is here at last, and the weather is warm and sunny today after the winds and rain of the past weeks.

The primroses are out and the apple trees are so pretty in the garden with their delicate pink and white blossom. The daffodils are fading and the bluebells have pushed through and will flower soon. Cow parsley grows so fast along the banks; you can almost watch it grow and it will soon be displaying its lace-like panicles of white along the roadsides and river banks.

The buds are bursting on the ash and the oak is not far behind. Do you know the old country saying?

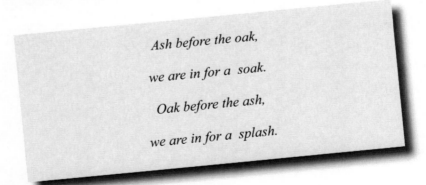

Ash before the oak,

we are in for a soak.

Oak before the ash,

we are in for a splash.

It could be that we are in for a wet summer then if this is true, but I do hope not.

Do you remember the first time we travelled to London? It was a weekend break, on a special offer from Saga magazine. How we caught the train from Southampton Parkway and you didn't realise how frequent they were; at least three in the hour, although it did make a difference which one to catch because some of them seemed to stop at every lamp post!

We managed to catch the fast train and find room for our cases close to our seat where we could look out of the window. This is important for you because you once had a case with valuable contents stolen while travelling to Scotland.

I had bought the current edition of the *Reader's Digest*, and we whiled away the time trying to guess the true meaning of the words in the 'Word Power' section. Between us we got them all right, so senility hasn't settled in just yet!

I was proudly wearing my new long black leather boots; the first pair I have ever been able to get into comfortably and do up the zips. The reason is that my legs are too fat, probably a result of too much sport, especially hockey, years ago; well, that's my excuse anyway.

We arrived on time at Waterloo and decided to take a taxi across London partly because of the cases, which are difficult to manage on the underground or on buses, and partly because we didn't know where we were going exactly.

We also had no idea how close the nearest underground station was to the hotel. It's not much fun dragging suitcases along London streets, even if they are on wheels. It makes such a din and you feel as though everyone is looking to see the cause of the racket; although I doubt if anyone notices in all the hustle and bustle which is the norm in Town.

The other important point was that we were going to the Hilton at Paddington, and I am sure it's not the 'done thing' to arrive by any form of public transport.

It's always easy to hire a cab at Waterloo; you just join the queue, so that is what we did and were soon speeding our way across London. It is great to travel by taxi because you get to see the sights and many famous places, and if I remember correctly, it was a fine day with the sun shining although quite cold.

Arriving at the hotel, the taxi driver opened the door and helped with the suitcases. We could see the red carpet on the steps, but I am sure it had not been put out especially for us (although it's fun to think it was). The doorman, resplendent in his uniform complete with top hat, was waiting to greet us and carry the cases. You climbed out first and I tried to follow with equal dignity, but I somehow tripped in my new boots and nearly fell headlong into the arms of the waiting doorman on the steps of the hotel. So much for fashion and long boots! The doorman kept a straight face, showed great concern and helped me to my feet, while you paid the taxi driver, giving him a generous tip, and we went into the hotel, to formally announce our arrival, without further mishap.

Our room was comfortable, and we decided to explore the surroundings and found that the hotel led straight onto Paddington station via a covered way and a shopping precinct.

We enjoyed some sushi at the Japanese raw fish bar before looking in the other shops, which included a mini mart. Here we bought some wine to drink in our room before dinner because the hotel prices are exorbitant for alcoholic drinks served at the bar and from the mini bar in the fridge.

Later, we were about to consume some of this fine liquor, to discover that the bottles had corks, not screw tops; and of course we had no corkscrew. Dilemma! After a brief discussion, I decided to go to the bar to ask to borrow a corkscrew from the bartender. He, perhaps surprisingly, was most sympathetic and accompanied me to the room to open the bottle for us. Maybe this is a more common practice than we thought, unless he was under the impression that this might be an invitation for other things!

At breakfast the following morning, there was a very good choice of food displayed in buffet style; both hot and cold dishes. Some were traditionally English with bacon, eggs, sausages, fried bread, toast and marmalade, etc. There was also a range of cereals and a large pot of porridge which to your dismay was virtually empty. I tried to persuade you to do without porridge for one morning and choose something else, but to no avail. Undeterred, you approached one of the waiters and, looking very down in the mouth and in your most gracious 'poor me' fashion, asked for more porridge. Dickens' Oliver could certainly take a leaf out of your book when wanting something which appears to be in short supply. Maybe you felt like the three bears discovering empty plates after Goldilocks had feasted on porridge.

Anyway, the obliging waiter was only too willing to help and you got fresh porridge to fortify you for the day. We both ate a hearty breakfast because it is part of the deal and because it meant we could have just a snack out before returning to the hotel for the 'all in' dinner.

We headed for Covent Garden on the underground. I knew this was a favourite place for you, but it was a first visit for me. We managed to get off at the right stop but had to ask the way even then because it is so easy to head in the wrong direction out of the tube and end up lost, as I have on more than one occasion in the capital!

Arriving at Covent Garden, we looked around the little shops and stood watching the street performers and musicians before having lunch on the lower level at the Crusting Pipe, a favourite pub of yours, to have a meal. I can understand why. It has a cosy atmosphere, good service, a varied menu and a range of fine wines, specialising in port. We had lunch inside because it was quite cold but we could hear the string quartet playing in the courtyard outside.

I have looked up some information on the name to discover that 'crusted' is a term used for a type of port. I thought it interesting so I am sharing my new-found info with you.

The name Crusting Pipe is significant because a 'pipe' is a barrel of port usually containing about 570 litres and a crusting pipe is a barrel of 'crusted port', and crusted port is so called because of the sediment which forms in the bottle.

It's supposed to be an economical alternative to vintage port because it is a blend of several harvests bottled without being filtered (hence the sediment, I guess) and then left to mature like vintage wines.

Funny how some wines last forever if stored properly and others change to vinegar relatively quickly, like the case of wine you found under your house. It was at least ten years old and you had no idea it was there until you needed some electrical work carried out and the electrician found it in the cellar. It will make good wine vinegar though; BJ and I have a vinegar 'plant' which we brought back from France. It does just that – changes old wine into vinegar with the help of bacteria in a 'mother plant' (no, not quite water into wine – at least I don't think so).

I remember visiting Madeira where the opposite is true. In the wine cellars there they have wines going back over a hundred years. It would be fun to buy one from the year you were born, wouldn't it? Although it might be a bit pricey and you might not like the taste of it anyway, so perhaps we'll give that a miss because I doubt if you could have a sample without paying for the whole bottle.

The label on crusted port indicates the year it was bottled, not the year of the harvest, so you wouldn't know how long it has been lying around and had things added to it. I suppose that doesn't matter if it tastes OK, and has the desired effect.

One manufacturer has described it as having an 'ethereal' quality, which according to the dictionary means 'very delicate, exquisite, highly refined, airy and heavenly'; that would certainly be a desired effect! Maybe we should try it sometime.

There were so many interesting little shops in Covent Garden, but perhaps one of the most unusual and unexpected finds was a little shop called Segar and Snuff which was quite close to the Crusting Pipe.

The Segar and Snuff Parlour is apparently one of London's last remaining tobacco specialists which has a selection of loose pipe tobaccos which can be blended to order.

There are also Havana cigars of every description and snuff! I remember my dad and uncles smoking a pipe and my brother smoking cigars. I loved the smell of them but now there's a major taboo on smoking in all public places because of all the connections with ill health, so I rarely have the opportunity to be nostalgic about the aroma.

One of my father's acquaintances used to take snuff, by placing a small amount on the back of his hand. With a hefty snort the snuff disappeared up his nostrils. As a small child I found this amazing and very funny, especially when this was followed by sneezing into a very large handkerchief. I am not sure even now what the desired effect was, but I'm sure there must have been one!

It was quite an adventure and a memorable one for us both.

Love, M

1st July 2006

Dear B

I haven't been to London to assess the managers for several months, but today I visited a day centre for older Afro-Caribbean people. It's one of my favourite places because they are always so cheerful and lively.

I was up early, and still in my dressing gown I watered the pots of tomatoes at the back so as not to wake the rest of the house. The puppies are impossible to get by quietly, so I had to let them out in the garden and clear up the smelly loose dump, no doubt produced by Max who has been slightly off his food, probably because he eats all sorts of rubbish. I think this habit probably applies to most dogs but I think is particularly true for Labradors.

Max has decided my comfy garden chair is the best place for him too. Oh well, today I was too busy to worry about it and he looked quite content. Just as long as he doesn't chew the arms it doesn't really matter!

I was not in too much of a rush today as I got ready for a day in London; I had time for a shower, washed my hair and walked the puppies round the field. I also had breakfast but no coffee (already I feel a visit to Bonapartes at Victoria coming on). At the station there was nearly a space for my car in the road and I risked being just over the line (parking has never been my strong point). I have never seen a traffic warden in Shoreham, but whether or not you are fined for parking in the wrong place depends how busy the 'Plods' are in the town.

I caught the train comfortably with five minutes to spare, and tried to do the Su Doku on the back page of the *times2*, but it took the whole journey and I still only completed half of it. There were too many distractions from a guy on a mobile phone organising his staff for the day and made all the more difficult for him as we went through tunnels in the Haywards Heath area. Well, that's my excuse anyway. I left the newspaper for someone cleverer than me to finish the puzzle – at least I've given the next person a head start! I always use a pencil for Su Doku because often I guess towards the end or if I get fed up, especially with the fiendish one, so that's an added advantage for anyone who spots a mistake and wants to complete it.

At Victoria I felt good and strode along, singing to myself; I ordered a coffee and cinnamon something at Bonapartes. The chairs are comfortable here, so I started to read the freebie newspaper, the *Metro*. Then I needed to go to the loo and followed the sign to the Ladies in the restaurant, forgetting you need a code for the key pad. A kind gentleman who was going to the Gents opposite saw my dilemma and said, "Shall I tap the code in for you?" and promptly did so, not waiting for a reply. It's only later that I thought, how does he know the code for the Ladies? Especially when he also came in with me, and showed me how to unlock the door! I said, "Thanks very much," and he promptly disappeared into the Gents opposite.

Oh well, just one of those things, I guess. Perhaps he was here with his wife or girlfriend and helped them out of the same predicament.

The No. 52 bus was waiting as always in Terminus Place, and I was still singing aloud to myself. The sun wasn't out in London, and I wished I'd brought a jacket even though it's summer. I discovered that sitting downstairs on the bus at the back is one way to keep warm. It must be near the engine because the seat was hot and also vibrated (no further comment on that!).

I enjoyed the ride along what is now a familiar route but just as I'm about to get off at Ladbroke Grove, I'm stuck because the man in the seat behind me has his great big foot on my skirt. Good job I'm not in a rush or I could have lost it altogether! (The skirt, that is.) He didn't realise until I tapped him on the shoulder and politely said, "Your foot's on my skirt." He was a youngish chap, dressed casually, and he grinned in response and said, "Sorry, luv." He moved his foot and I went on my way, but he waved cheekily to me from the bus window as it moved off.

When I reflected on what might have happened, I'm glad I was wearing clean frilly knickers. Well, that could have been thrilling for other folks on the bus if I had lost my skirt! I'm sure the young guy with his size 10s would have been further amused.

I bet he exaggerates the story when he gets to work or in the pub tonight and has me throwing myself into his arms or something. I wonder if he did it on purpose.

I hadn't been to this centre for a while and I had to really think about which way to go as I stood on the pavement by the bus stop. After surveying the scene I crossed the road and walked along the passageway. My student wasn't there – he had gone out on the minibus to collect up the old folk. That was a relief; I had time to finish entering the evidence in his portfolio before he came back. Sometimes I am quite sure 'someone up there' organises these things and enables me to get all my work done comfortably. I've stopped worrying about it, and that same 'someone' sure does take care of my diary and workload.

My student returned and had bought me a souvenir from China. I was very touched by this – it's a mobile that you can hang up and it has Chinese patterns all over it. He has enjoyed his visit to his son and daughter in China and told me I should go for a visit. He said his son would take me places and that he speaks Cantonese. Mmm… perhaps one day?

The day went well; my student has nearly completed the course but he was tired (a bit jet-lagged still, I think) and so I arranged another date and left him some questions to complete before my next visit.

I decided to go back to Victoria on the No. 52 bus and just look out for interesting people and things. Here are some of them:

A cinema with a film called *All About My Mother*. I think I could also make an interesting film about mine. Could you make one about yours?

We have just passed the Royal Albert Hall, where the Proms are currently playing. One of my ambitions is to go to the last night there. I love all the pomp and circumstance stuff on that night. Perhaps one day I will be able to go and join in.

A protest outside Hyde Park and I craned forward to see what it was all about. There were lots of home-made banners and people chanting and shouting. It seemed to be about releasing political prisoners but I couldn't see where exactly – guess it's to do with the war in Iraq or something.

Then past Grosvenor Square, the spelling of that drives me mad. I always want to say Grovesnor, which would make a lot more sense. What or who is a Grosvenor anyway? Something else to investigate further.

I caught the train home without much of a wait. It was lurching all over the place and I wondered how it stays on its tracks. It must have had loose suspension or something, so I had a cup of coffee from the trolley to steady my nerves. Balancing it and actually drinking it was quite a feat! Every time I tried to take a sip, the train seemed to speed round a bend or braked sharply thus resulting in coffee spilling all over the book I was reading. I was glad when we reached Shoreham without any further mishap. That's it!

Love, M

PS. I have arrived home and looked up info about Grosvenor Square, and as always places in London have an interesting and exciting history (as do most places in Town) and are not boring at all. I will certainly look at it in a different light each time I pass it and pronounce the name correctly. I am sure it will be worth a visit one day.

Grosvenor Square

Firstly, the pronunciation is Grovenor with a silent S - this important fact could save embarrassment in the future if we need to ask directions or take a cab to it! Knowing the correct pronunciation for London place names could also prevent us being identified quite as readily as country yokels.

Anyway, the name is the family name of the Dukes of Westminster, who have an impressive pedigree with a history stretching back to Norman times when Gilbert le Grosveneur came to England with William the Conqueror as chief huntsman. Quite a successful story of successive generations rising through the ranks from huntsman to Dukedom!

The Grosvenor family have an interesting motto - 'Virtus non stemma'.

This literally means 'Virtue not lineage' but in everyday language translates as: 'It is what you do that matters, not who your ancestors were.' I think that's a great motto; perhaps I'll adopt it as my own.

Anyway, apparently, in 1710 Sir Richard Grosvenor (6th Baronet) developed Grosvenor Square and so it became a place of fashionable houses until the Second World War.

Grosvenor Square also has an important connection with the USA; it currently houses the American Embassy. John Adams, the first United States Minister to the Court of St James's and the second President of the United States, lived there from 1785 to 1788 and General Eisenhower's headquarters were based there in the Second World War. Then Grosvenor Square became popularly known as 'Little America'.

There are also two other memorial statues erected; one here to President Roosevelt and the other to President Eisenhower. A bronze sculpture of the American Bald Eagle mounted on a shaft of white Portland stone is also to be found here to commemorate the Eagle Squadron. The latter were the pilots of the American Eagle Squadron who volunteered to join the British Air Force during the war.

The most recent memorial is a garden remembering those people who tragically lost their lives in the United States on 11th September 2001. The garden has been planted with white roses. These are significant because the Queen included them in her tribute to the people killed, and do you remember the first anniversary of this in St Paul's Cathedral when white rose petals were cascaded from the ceiling in remembrance? I think that is such a touching and sensitive symbol.

I hope you find the history of Grosvenor Square as fascinating and interesting as I do.

LETTER 6.

11th November 2006

Dear B

I haven't seen you for ages although we have spoken on the phone and sent text messages via mobiles.

Today is a typical foggy November day; the mist will probably stay in the valley here all day. I have walked the dogs along the riverbank because they have to go out whatever the weather. There wasn't much to see today in the mist but the dogs don't care; they are still able to sniff out a dead fish or horse dung to roll in.

Max tugged at my sleeve anyway as soon as I finished breakfast. This has become a habit with him. He and Bruno wolf down their own breakfast and then watch enviously while I eat my cereal. As soon as the last mouthful is consumed and I put down my spoon, this signals a call for action and a reminder that they have not yet had a walk. Sometimes dogs are too intelligent for my liking and, in instances like this, train their owner rather than vice versa!

Anyway, they have had a walk and are now asleep in the lounge so I thought I would write to you. Fortunately, I do not have to travel to London today in this dreary weather, although I guess fog would be an improvement on the smog of the 1950s.

I was thinking today about some of our visits to London and found myself reminiscing about my student experiences there. I thought you might be interested in some of these tales of misspent youth!

I travelled from Somerset into Paddington, across London to Liverpool Street station then to college in Cambridge as a student (plus heavy cases). The trains were always crowded then and it was easier to just sit on the case in the corridor. That would be difficult with the modern rolling stock but there seem to be fewer students with luggage these days – I think maybe parents collect them by car. My trunk, an essential piece of equipment, was always sent on the railways ahead, packed with clothes and goodies, including home-made chocolate cakes, and books.

I was always surprised that the London buses were red; at home in Somerset they were green. I also found it odd that the locations of stations were in the middle of busy streets in the city. I was used to stations on the outskirts of town and the need for a bus journey or long walk to get to them.

The size and grandness of the buildings were always and still are impressive. In Wellington the tallest buildings were the Town Hall (in the centre of town) and the dentist's house, just three storeys high, along the High Street! I used to find the busyness, hustle and bustle of London a bit overwhelming and rushed along with the crowd who always seemed in such a hurry to get some place. These days I am much more laid-back and try to go at my own pace – always much easier, especially if it's not the rush hour. The amount of traffic hasn't changed much in spite of the introduction of the congestion charge in recent years.

While I was still at college I spent one summer holiday in London as a nanny to four children in St John's Wood. That's how I came to know more about the capital and find my way around it. I took the children to the cinema to see *Mary Poppins* and *The Sound of Music* and later, on holiday, we had great fun at Rock in Cornwall as we danced over the sand dunes, singing the lyrics from them.

I spent New Year with a friend in London once and did all the daft things students do, like shopping at Harrods for sweets just to get a bag with the logo on the outside; visiting numerous pubs but resisting the temptation to smoke hash. Cigarettes were a status symbol for any self-respecting student, and we drank Mateus rosé wine so we could keep the green flat-shaped bottles and put candles in the top for evenings in when we played canasta, sometimes all night. Her fiancé arrived unexpectedly on the Saturday evening at her basement flat, so I had to move discreetly to the kitchen end of the corridor so that I didn't play gooseberry and disturb their romantic evening.

I was too 'chicken' to jump in the fountain at midnight as Big Ben struck on New Year's Eve while Nelson, guarded by his lions, looked down from his tall column disapprovingly, or was it with envy?

On a different occasion I arrived in Waterloo from Southampton at midnight, having spent the weekend with a friend which ended in a row. There were no onward trains because it was Sunday, and the only alternative to sleeping on the streets was to be locked in the ladies' waiting room and sleep on the table.

I was encouraged to do the latter by two burly policemen on the station who were checking all the down-and-outs. It was an uncomfortable night, and in the morning I wandered around looking for a place to get a drink; I think I only had a little money, enough to buy a coffee. I felt like a down-and-out myself, which probably spurred me on to help with Crisis at Christmas one year. Clearing up afterwards, I began to itch and found I had flea bites. The only other time I had fleas was when I was teaching in Devon and caught them from the school chicken, but that's another story!

I'm sure you wanted to know all that, but it is fun to reflect sometimes on all the things one did in one's youth, misspent or not!

Love, M

LETTER 7.

12th November 2006

Dear B

Another trip to London which didn't start too well...

I slept late and felt thick-headed so was a bit dim trying to get ready. I spent too long trying to do a Su Doku and left myself half an hour to shower, dress and organise my briefcase.

I couldn't find the handbag with my Oyster card in. "For goodness' sake," I said to my sister (who is staying with us), "it's a huge bag, navy blue in colour." In usual practical fashion, she suggests, "When did you last have it? You might have left it somewhere," but I know I haven't and went tearing round the house like a mad thing trying to find it. Then I remembered I tidied up my room after all the ironing in the past two days – so where was it? Why of course! There it was hanging up neatly behind the bedroom door. (I never do that – hanging things up, like I never do ironing!)

I rushed out of the house, opening the garage door on the remote button (one of the best innovations of the twentieth century, in my opinion). This invention means I no longer have to leap at the door to make it stay up, and prevent it falling back on my head. My sister kindly offered to open the gate for me, and I nearly ran her over as I hastily reversed out of the drive. I had 15 minutes to get to the station. Should be plenty of time, I told myself, but I had to buy my ticket and hoped I had enough change for the car park. There was, of course, more traffic than usual heading out of the village, so I was delayed at the first roundabout and forced to follow a slow-moving lorry to Shoreham flyover. All the time I was frantically working out how long it should take at this speed to go the four miles to the station. At the roundabout I heaved a sigh of relief – good! Most of the traffic went left to

Brighton, and I was going right. But wait a minute, there was a queue of traffic at the next roundabout, which was not moving. Some car driver had broken down right on the roundabout. I muttered to myself about people with old cars and not having them fixed regularly, but eventually, we all squeezed by on the other side of the road. Six minutes to go – this was really cutting it fine, and I groaned inwardly, trying to tell myself, it's OK, and maybe part of some higher plan.

I whizzed down the side street, and fortunately the school crossing patrol was not yet on duty on the pavement. I parked quickly, and for once had enough change for the ticket. Three minutes to go, as I ran out of the car park, onto the platform to buy a rail ticket at the automatic machine, which is fortunately working. Wait a minute! The machine decided not to print me a ticket even though it accepted my bank card and pin. There was now a queue of people behind me, all getting frustrated and looking dubiously at me. It crossed my mind that they are probably thinking that I've no money in the account! I ignored them and tried again. This time it worked and the machine spat out a ticket just as the train drew alongside the platform. (I hope I haven't been charged twice for this ticket!) I resolved to organise my life so that I buy a ticket in advance in future.

I walked smartly along the side of the train, to get as near the front as possible, so that there wasn't so far to walk at Victoria. Boarding the train, I was pleased to get a window seat with two spare seats beside me, and I sat down still slightly out of breath. Phew! Made it! I felt a little brighter and noticed that the sun was shining. I put my case on the overhead rack, making sure that the handle was sticking out, so I can reach it later. I sat back and relaxed, and began to people watch and observed my travelling companions.

Gloom descended again as I noticed opposite me a very smart, well-dressed couple. I can tell they haven't got up in a hurry, lost handbags, raced to the station and fought with the ticket machine. They both have co-ordinating outfits and I was very aware that my red handbag and jacket and shoes are all different shades of red. The woman had put on make-up and was obviously practised at it – me? I was wearing none but I decided against putting it on then and there. I just knew they would think it a little infra dig. The woman's nails were well manicured, and I tried to hide my cracked nails, which were badly in need of treatment, in my lap. Her hair was well cut, and I was suddenly aware that my fringe was creeping down over my nose, and I hadn't had it cut since I was in France six weeks ago. I resolved to make an appointment tomorrow.

The man with her (husband for sure) had a straight parting, and I had a sudden urge to ruffle his hair. But I resisted this action, and just gazed innocently out of the window.

I could see she was reading a potted version of *The Da Vinci Code*, which eventually sent her to sleep. He was reading some boring magazine from the Sunday paper (no, not *The Tatler* as one might expect). I tried to listen when they occasionally spoke to each other, but it was all very *sotto voce*. She then gets out Tic Tacs and they both discreetly suck on them, so I assumed she had asked him if he wanted a sweet. I have an overwhelming desire to chew gum – so I dug a flattened packet out of my pocket and found the last cracked bit. It's difficult to chew gum surreptitiously but I did nevertheless, sure that my travelling companions would not condescend to such a habit.

Further down the line she sneezed and of course had a handkerchief (a clean one) to hand. Funny how I had the same urge to sneeze but could only find a very old tissue in my pocket, which came to light after dragging out a 'doggie bag' and a handful of crumby dog biscuits left over from my walk with Max and Bruno. Well, the tissue had to do. I really didn't feel I could use my sleeve! I really was feeling like a country bumpkin. At the next stop I am cheered by a young guy who boarded the train and sat opposite me. He was in his mid twenties, I guess. He was handsome, rugged and with a pleasant face, and I dreamed of being 35 years younger, remembering the romantic story I read yesterday in the paper. It was about the successful partnership of an older woman and her 'toy boy' friend… well, it was in the USA!

I continued to regard the couple opposite, who refused to make eye contact of any kind; perhaps they thought I was a figment of their imagination or something. They started muttering about coffee, and I thought me too. I couldn't wait to get to Victoria and have a cappuccino and apple Danish at Bonapartes.

A young girl joined the train at the next stop and gave me a broad smile, so I knew I really do exist and maybe was half human after all. The final icing on the cake was that the handsome young man waited while I collected my case and put on my coat. Then he graciously let me get out into the aisle, holding up Mr and Mrs Neat 'n' Tidy. I just loved that guy!

Passing through the ticket barrier and across the station concourse, I crossed London on the No. 52 bus, which was driven by a maniac hurtling along at what felt like twice the speed limit. It left me wondering if bus lanes are a good idea after all. I eventually arrived at my destination, having got off two stops too early and had to walk a long way down the road because I wasn't sure where I would end up! Oh well, tomorrow is another day and today can only get better, I thought as I entered the building for a day's work.

On the return journey, on the No. 52 bus hurtling through London again, I sat on the upper deck of the bus because I enjoy the views out of the window and like to identify the famous places and reflect on past visits to them. I managed to get a seat at the front, having staggered up the stairs as the bus started off and swayed into the seat.

At the moment we are passing Hyde Park and we have exchanged text messages about standing on soap boxes at Speaker's Corner. You have challenged me to make a speech here, promising that if I do you will come and heckle. It's a tempting challenge, but I cannot think of any burning issues that I want to proclaim from a soap box in Hyde Park at the moment. Anyway, I think you can only do this on Sunday. Perhaps next time we have a weekend in London we could go and see who is saying what about what and both heckle! I wonder how it all started.

Love, M

PS. I am now home and have looked up some interesting info about the history of Hyde Park.

Hyde Park

Until the sixteenth century Hyde Park belonged to the monks of Westminster Abbey; then Henry VIII, no less, took it over so that he could hunt deer. So it stayed as a royal hunting ground until James I appointed a keeper to look after the park. (Perhaps it had become a right royal mess!)

Everything changed during the reign of Charles I, who opened the park to the general public, and when the Great Plague hit London, people tried to escape the city by camping there.

Later in the same century William III introduced 300 oil lamps to be set up through the park as a safety measure. I think these must have been the first street lamps in England. For some reason he found it scary travelling between Kensington Palace and St James's – maybe there were highwaymen or vagabonds about, but I'm sure he had a guard of some sort.

Anyway, this route became known as the 'King's Route' or in French (which was spoken by any respectable person at that time) 'Route de Roi'. Over the years this has somehow become changed (I guess by increasingly bad pronunciation and the decline of French as a second language) to 'Rotten Row'. I think he might be quite upset by this degradation if he knew!

In the 1730s the Serpentine was created by Queen Caroline, wife of George II, and after that Hyde Park was used as a venue for national celebrations – for example:

In 1814 the Prince Regent organised fireworks to mark the end of the Napoleonic wars;

The Great Exhibition during the reign of Queen Victoria which celebrated the achievements of industry, arts and innovation worldwide;

In 1977 a Silver Jubilee Exhibition was held in honour of Queen Elizabeth II's 25 years on the throne, and for her Golden Jubilee, a gun salute by the King's Troop Royal Horse Artillery.

And finally, Speaker's Corner!

You probably know that this was originally the site where many people were hanged for a variety of offences (whether genuine or contrived). Before meeting their doom they were allowed a final speech to the often very large crowd.

Samuel Pepys (1664), an observer on at least one occasion, records in his diary an estimated crowd of 12,000–14,000 people. It was much later that an Act of Parliament passed in 1872 (The Royal Parks and Gardens Regulation Act) allowed a space in the north-eastern corner of Hyde Park to be given over for public speaking. This then made the site official for public speaking even though it had been used for that purpose for hundreds of years, since the spectacle of public hanging moved to Newgate Prison in 1759.

I think I will just stick to writing rather than speaking, anyway.

I so enjoy finding out more about London; my historical knowledge is sadly lacking.

That's all for now. Hope to catch up with you soon.

LETTER 8.

14ᵗʰ November 2006

Dear B

This is another of those funny kinda days.

I awoke feeling tired; I think I will stop taking sleeping tablets, which I have had while I have been ill. BJ had gone to work and the house was quiet. I wandered into the lounge and picked up *The Times* and sat down to do the Su Doku. I did this in five minutes and texted the answer, hoping to win £1,000!

I looked down at my feet to see I am wearing one black shoe and one slipper! Senior moment or what? Well, they feel comfortable, so no need to change.

I took Max and Bruno to Bramber Castle and walked round the moat; the dogs so enjoy running up and down the sides and then chasing rabbits at the top. Fortunately they rarely catch one; if they do, Bruno has to eat his prey which takes him about 15 minutes; bones, fur, the whole lot disappears. Max is quite happy to give anything he catches to me and I can throw it somewhere out of reach.

You will probably be relieved to hear that I was wearing matching boots as I left the house! And the journey to the station was uneventful for once. I managed to park in the car park but have parked so close to a lamp post I couldn't easily get my coat out! But there was no time to move it and the car park was full anyway.

The train to Victoria was late so I caught the train to Brighton. The automatic TVs were all down there so I had no clue what train to get on – so I had to ask! As you know, I don't like doing this and it is always a last resort to find out information. The station staff always seem to look at me as though I am some kind of dimwit, and so I usually end up speaking like one.

I took the train to King's Cross, which was better because it stopped at Kensington Olympia right near where I want to go. It's a new place, so I had to find my way right to the end of Kensington High Street with the help of a street map! The writing was a bit small and it's quite old though, so I thought I might have to ask someone again for directions.

I had just had a call on my mobile while on the train, but the call was cut short by going through a tunnel!

Cor! This was a rickety, old-fashioned train and I kept making loads of 'seplping msitkes'!

Today there were three teenagers in the compartment, 18ish, chatting to each other.

'Annihilated' seems to be a new word in their vocabulary, which apparently means getting drunk. Cricket, mobile phones and barbecues are also the key topics of conversation.

One lad described his body as a 'temple' because he hadn't drunk alcohol all weekend. Interesting!

He was trying to grow a beard. The other two lads were wearing loose ¾ trousers and tee shirts with collars, in which they looked quite smart. The usual phrases used by young people such as: 'cool', 'wicked', 'like' spattered the conversation in ways I don't understand but which I find fascinating! The young girl commented that her friend is going out with an older guy. The lads thought this weird because she is still at school and they no longer looked at schoolgirls. One of them said that maybe it is for companionship. (Mmm... what else would it be?)

My travelling companions changed to commuters casually dressed, so I listened for clues as to possible vocation. They were all reading the freebie newspaper but have copies of the *Guardian* as well. Is that a clue? I read the freebie on the station because I was early. Can you believe that the only interesting bit of news is an earthquake in Folkestone! Did you see it on the news? It reminded me of the time when I lived in Dover back in the Sixties. I was awoken by a huge bang one Saturday morning in the early hours and the whole house shook. I had a flat on the third floor and was quite scared because my flatmate was away for the weekend, as were the other folks in the house. An earthquake? A bomb? I had no idea and all sorts of things raced through my mind so I rang the telephone operator to find out what had happened (all calls went through the operator back then because Dover was not yet on STD). Two ships had collided in the English Channel very close to the cliffs, and the reverberation must have travelled through the land. Well, that was a relief, I can tell you, and fortunately the house was not damaged.

Oh no, the train has just come to a halt in a tunnel near Haywards Heath. A message is coming over the tannoy. We stopped here, apparently, because the bridge ahead had just been bashed by a large vehicle trying to go under it! I am so glad it is safe; we could have been there a looooong time! (We are now on the move again.) It's a beautiful spring morning, but can you believe that last night in church we were praying for rain!? The local farmer had been planting maize on the hill above Beeding, and he described it as a dust bowl and that the crop would be awful this year if the seed managed to grow at all! We have had only four per cent of the average rainfall for April this year. Yesterday in the garden we filled the water butts with the hose. BJ finds it too difficult to carry watering cans very far and the hose doesn't reach some parts of the garden.

I feel very relaxed today and have been thinking about our most recent weekend in London. I think one of the most impressive places we have visited is St Paul's Cathedral. I thought you might like to share the information I have found out about St Paul's Cathedral. We learnt such a lot that day and I have since looked up the website of St Paul's to find out more about it. It's amazing to think that there has been a cathedral here since 604 and that this is the fourth building built by Sir Christopher Wren following the Great Fire of London in 1666. It took 35 years to complete the rebuild, which was funded by an increased tax on coal! The dome is the second largest in the world. The largest is of course in St Peter's Basilica in Rome. Both domes are based on the one in the Pantheon built by the ancient Romans. I think it is very fitting that Sir Christopher Wren is the first person to be buried here, when he died in 1723.

It really is a church which reflects the history of the country down through the ages with art, carvings and architecture from each generation. I find it interesting that Queen Victoria thought that the cathedral was 'dreary and dingy' and so mosaics were added at her request to brighten up the interior. The record of worshippers and events here is most impressive including both sad occasions, such as the funeral services of Lord Nelson and Sir Winston Churchill, and jubilant celebrations, the latter including the eightieth and hundredth birthdays of Queen Elizabeth The Queen Mother; the wedding of Prince Charles to Lady Diana Spencer; and, most recently, the thanksgiving services for both the Golden Jubilee and eightieth birthday of Her Majesty The Queen. Although the cathedral was bombed during the Second World War, the damage has been repaired.

St Paul's for many years has been a place where people can debate current affairs. This used to take place in the churchyard by St Paul's cross. More recently, this tradition has been revived and thousands have gathered inside St Paul's to join in debates of present-day issues. Anyone can join these debates from any religious belief or none and eminent speakers have included Kofi Anan, the Archbishop of Canterbury, Rowan Williams, Baroness Shirley Williams, Sir David Attenborough and Gordon Brown.

The topic for autumn 2009 is 'For richer, for poorer: how money shapes our lives' and will debate how money shapes our world for good or ill. In the current economic climate you can't get more topical than that, can you!?

We are now arriving at Victoria, so more news later.

Today the bus has taken me along past Hyde Park, the Royal Albert Hall and Harrods. Harrods! Do you remember shopping there on our last trip to London? It really is an amazing experience but most of the things on sale are outside our income bracket. It's always fun to look around, though, and have a snack in the food hall. I always buy something just so I can have a Harrods bag to walk around London with to impress people, including family and friends when I get home. Usually it only has a pen or sweets inside but it makes me feel good!

I think you bought some presents for your family, a kitchen apron, tea towel and oven gloves all with the Harrods crest on them. I hope the recipients were suitably impressed!

Harrods has changed radically throughout its history. I was interested to read the other day on their website that it was a store opened by one Henry Harrod in the inner city in 1834 at Stepney in the East End. It transferred to Knightsbridge in 1851 to get away from the filth of the inner city. I think its close proximity to Hyde Park was an advantage and also the forthcoming event of the Great Exhibition planned for 1851.

Although it burnt down in 1883, the store has both survived and thrived until present time. The fire occurred just before Christmas but somehow, I think with great determination, the Christmas orders were all delivered on time (I guess by horse and cart), and the store made a profit to boot!

It wasn't long after this that credit was offered to its more affluent customers, such as the playwright Oscar Wilde and the actress Ellen Terry. That's a bit different from today, isn't it, when virtually anyone can have credit whether affluent or not? The family firm became a public company in 1889, and the following decade was a highly successful period which included the very first winter clearance sale. The building of the first escalator in the world followed. To prevent any undue trauma or stress from this new experience, customers were offered brandy on reaching the top. I wonder when that idea fell out of fashion but perhaps people abused the system – sounds like an excellent practice to me!

It has always sold a wide variety of merchandise from pets (Noel Coward bought an alligator and A. A. Milne purchased the original Winnie the Pooh bear for his son Christopher) to fresh herrings flown direct to Alfred Hitchcock in Hollywood. The store also offered a range of services. Sigmund Freud was embalmed by Harrods (part of the funeral arrangements) and it was possible to hire a fully equipped ambulance plus nurse or arrange for your clock to be wound up. Amazing!

You could also live above the store in a luxury apartment in the 1920s; now that would be an address to have, wouldn't it?!

They really live up to their motto 'Everything for everybody everywhere'.

LETTER 9.

30th April 2007

Dear B

Another trip to London to 'Hot Stuff Home' (so called because they always have pepper sauce on the tables at lunchtime!).

On the seats around me today are school lads in their early teens, who still have to wear uniform (reluctantly, I think). One is quiet, the other two chatty. The smallest, the most talkative lad, says that looking out of the window is so boring. I think the beauty of the Sussex countryside with open green fields, woodlands, tiled houses and the backdrop of the Downs is not appreciated by him somehow!

He would like to work at a station, he says, but gives no reason and there is no comment from the other two. They are enjoying arm wrestling, which to me appears a hopeless situation for the smaller of the two lads. But I guess he has to try.

We have just stopped at Portslade, and two girls have rushed through to get off the train because there is a short platform here. "Hurry up, you dozy cow," says one as they rush through the carriage. I guess this is the language of youngsters today because I can't recall using that particular expression myself as a teenager! One of the lads suggests pushing the emergency button because that will hold the train at the station and give them time to get off. The other lad replies that this would be a good idea because they would be late for school. Such enthusiasm for education! I think Tony Blair would be disappointed with their attitude, but I expect it's the teachers' fault for failing to motivate them sufficiently; or maybe the parents are to blame by lack of support for their children. Who knows?

The other passengers are probably businessmen of various descriptions and they ignore me as well as everyone else in the carriage. One seems to find the freebie newspaper absorbing (probably the football disaster for Liverpool in Italy last night), and the other is working on papers taking up the desk space between us, so I move at the earliest moment for more room to use my laptop!

Summer is definitely here with open-necked shirts and short sleeves – I expect cotton boxer shorts, as underwear, are also the order of the day as opposed to long johns (or are the latter a thing of my father's generation?).

Hair growth at least to a number two cut is back in vogue, except for one guy who joins the train at Hassocks with long, straggly grey hair. He also has an equally straggly grey beard. He's out of breath and collapses into his seat, so not a good start to the morning for him. I feel for him, having only just caught the train so many times myself. He has a bottle of water with him and brings out headphones with an iPod. So I think he must be quite 'hip', even if he is middle aged. He is reading the *Telegraph*, so probably is not a socialist which destroys my idea of him as an ancient hippie. I would expect him to at least read the *Guardian*!

I thought about Helen travelling daily by train, and was glad that I don't have to do that! She used to overhear conversations too, and wonders why mobile phones were considered thoughtless by some passengers, while others don't mind. She told me about a conversation about a mobile phone user discussing contraception and the Catholic Church, but was unable to hear more because it was drowned out by two people comparing what they had eaten for breakfast.

On another occasion, she was sitting with some girls from Hong Kong, and although they couldn't speak English, they produced a camera and insisted that they had their photographs taken with her. We both wondered what tale they would tell on their return home about the 'older' person they had met on the train.

I wanted to catch the early train but for various reasons this didn't happen.

There were no car parking spaces on the road today outside the station, so I parked in the station car park with my £3 ready for the machine. It was out of order and so was the second one I tried. It will be interesting to see the outcome of this when I get back – maybe a £60 fine which of course I will refute. Maybe a wheel clamp; maybe nothing – hope it's the latter! After a busy day in London that's the last thing you want!

I bought my rail ticket from the machine on the station without any problem then found I had left my Oyster card at home – that's OK; the money for the car park will pay the bus fare although bus drivers in London, in my experience, dislike payment with real money!

There was no further excitement on the journey to Victoria and I was able to quietly get on with preparing questions for students. It's good news today that my student has finished collecting evidence for his portfolio, but bad news that I have to lug them all the way home by public transport! The No. 52 bus stopped at the beginning of Hyde Park and "Everyone change here" came the repeated announcement over the tannoy. Oh what?! We were getting on so well, lurching through London at a rate of knots. I patiently got off last so as not to bash into anyone with my briefcase and large carrier bag with the two portfolios, which are quite heavy. I had already taken off my cardigan, and stuffed that with my handbag into the overlarge carrier bag so as not to have too many bits to carry. I'm quite good at losing one piece of luggage when I have more than one bag to carry or at leaving one of them in unlikely places.

I never wear my specs in London for that reason, and anyway they fall off my nose quite readily at the moment since the dog has had several attempts at sharpening his teeth on them!

I was sure another No. 52 bus would be along shortly – but no, not a sign of one. Buses of every other number except mine came and went, sometimes three in a row, sometimes half empty. I asked myself, why didn't these buses unload and zoom off into the distance as mine had done? After 20 minutes: hooray, a No. 52 bus at last! So I staggered on with the carrier bag and briefcase and, once seated, decide to get my return train ticket ready for the barrier at Victoria, in case I have to hurry to catch the train.

Uh oh! My next problem was I had no pockets in the two piece I was wearing, so I discreetly tucked my ticket into my bra for safety, hoping it won't fall out when I bend over to pick up the luggage again. I decided this was a better idea than when as a child at school it was customary to keep handkerchiefs and other objects in one's knicker leg (anyway, they were large then – the knickers, I mean).

On arriving at Victoria, I was pleased that there was a fast train to Brighton in 15 minutes, and it's usually quicker to go home by this route. This gave me time to walk across the station and retrieve the ticket discreetly from its hiding place. I found a window seat on the train at a table which has plenty of room for my laptop. I idled away the time playing card games on the computer because I felt 'brain dead' and didn't want to think about work anymore today.

Having enjoyed a Kit Kat from the trolley service, I brushed the crumbs from my chest to discover I have a pocket in the suit top after all. All that discretion and anxiety about where to keep the ticket handy for nothing!

A train to Hove was waiting at Brighton so I heaved my bags off the train, walked round to the neighbouring platform and heaved them onto the next one. This performance was repeated at Hove where I changed to the slow train to Shoreham. I think it would have been easier to have waited for the through train from Victoria but I am always keen to travel home by the fastest possible route. So easy to be wise in hindsight! Arriving at Shoreham, I crossed the road outside the station only to cross back again, remembering that I had left my car in the station car park where the ticket machine was not working. Fortunately no wheel clamp or parking ticket awaited me and the machine is still out of order. I breathed a sigh of relief and drove home slowly, pleased that the London adventure is over for another day. Hope you enjoy this tale of the city – it's just as it happened.

Take care.

Love, M

LETTER 10.

24th May 2007

Dear B

All this train travel plus a journey on a steam train has led me to think back to my first encounter with trains.

I thought about the first time I travelled on a train. It would have been a steam train then, with old-fashioned carriages; I remember the leather straps which opened and closed the windows and the seats were all in compartments facing each other. The luggage racks were all overhead and the guard's van held all sorts of other luggage, including pets and extra-large suitcases. The trains were waved off by the guard's green flag and he blew a whistle.

Today it seems to be red batons which are held up by the station staff, which isn't half as much fun. I remember one time we all went on holiday as a family to Dunster Beach, on the train from Taunton station.

I was so interested in your first memory of travelling by train, B; that because your father worked on the railway you had free passes. You remember him carrying you on his shoulders to the station and watching the 'enormous' steam train come in hooting, clanking and puffing. You think you must have been about four years old and remembered how your mother had a little bag with sandwiches and your swimsuit and you went for the day to Felixstowe to spend a day by the sea. Here's the quote I have in my journal about that day:

> *I sat quietly in the carriage, wide-eyed at everything
> and was intrigued by the red chain and sign which said:*

ALARM SIGNAL TO STOP THE TRAIN IN CASE OF EMERGENCY
PULL DOWN THE CHAIN; PENALTY FOR IMPROPER USE £50

> *My only understanding of pulling a chain is going to the*
> *toilet, so I was scared that if I went to the toilet on the*
> *train and pulled the flush that the train would stop and*
> *I knew my parents hadn't got £50. My dad smoked his*
> *pipe and wore his trilby hat. On the beach he took off*
> *his collar and stud, rolled up his trousers showing his*
> *white legs after taking off the socks held up by suspend-*
> *ers. My mother's bag contained an empty flask because*
> *we could queue outside the local hotel for a pennyworth*
> *of boiling water to fill it!*
>
> *Later, during the Second World War, this was not pos-*
> *sible because the beach was cordoned off with barbed*
> *wire to prevent would-be invaders landing.*

Felixstowe, unlike the station in my hometown, which closed in 1964 under the Beeching Plan, is still a busy station, forming the terminus on the branch line for passengers from Ipswich and important in carrying freight trains to the port there.

We both have different recollections of these steam trains with no corridors, the overhead luggage racks and leather straps to open windows and doors. People leant out of the window when approaching a station, getting off before the train stopped and walking with the train so as not to fall over. Catching a train could be equally hazardous if people were late, running alongside the moving train and opening the doors to get on. The guard was too busy at this point, blowing his whistle and waving his green flag, to do anything about it. The handles were on the outside of the train. Today there are no handles at all so it would be impossible these days. The doors are automatic, closing one minute before the train pulls out, and not opening on arrival at a station for 30 seconds.

I have always been fascinated by trains from an early age when I used to go 'train spotting' at the local station with a friend. You were allowed on the platforms in those days (mid 1950s) before the advent of fast diesel trains and the introduction of at least a thousand and one health and safety regulations. I guess there were not so many trains too and fewer people travelling.

Life generally was also more laid-back and the hustle and bustle of London stations certainly not in evidence here. We used to watch the trains come in and note the names of the engines and watch people getting on and off. It must have been most unpleasant on rainy or cold days to have to put your head out of the window to open the doors. Usually the porters were ready to open doors and carry luggage for you but a tip was essential. There were always porters about too who kept the platform clean, picking up the rubbish, although there was not much of that (mainly cigarette butts, I think), and sweeping the platform with a very large broom. It was possible to watch the signalman in his box, manually pulling on the long-handled levers to move the points on the line and operate the signals. Sometimes if there was a long gap between trains we were allowed into the signal box for a short while to talk to the signalman. It meant climbing up some steep steps at the side to reach the box. It was such fun to watch the signal suddenly drop as a train approached and then jerk sharply up again once it had gone past. So much of the safe operation of the railways relied on manpower rather than automation.

We were able to watch the engines being topped up with water from the tanks high on the side of the line at one end of the platform. The fast trains en route to Paddington from Penzance didn't stop at the station but slowed down so that the mail bag could be hurled by the guard on the train into a large net which was slung between two poles at one end of the platform. There was a siding too where the engines were kept for maintenance. Occasionally we were allowed to get up beside the driver and stoker and chug up and down the siding. We stood well back and watched as they shovelled coal into the furnace inside which it was glowing red hot and smelt awful. Sometimes we would stand on the bridge outside the station and watch the trains come in and out with equal enjoyment, waving at the passengers rather like the Railway Children.

There's nothing quite like the smell of a steam train, is there, or the sound of the engine chugging along; the puffing of steam in long plumes from the funnel; and the clanking of the pistons turning the wheels. Goods trains were always interesting too as they rattled through and we tried to guess what they were carrying; sometimes it was obvious because of the open trucks, like those carrying coal.

I don't remember any fuss about trains not being on time but I guess there must have been times when they were late; I only know about one unusual occasion recounted to me by a friend: JM remembers her father banging his head on the door window when trying to get out, not realising the window was shut. He managed to break the glass and the train was held up while the window was repaired. I wonder how often that happened to passengers. She also recalls an overseas visitor who, wanting to alight at a station, couldn't find the door handle so climbed out of the window, not realising the handle was on the outside. What fun it was back then, or were we just too young to appreciate the problems or see the dangers? When the station closed under the Beeching Plan in the 1960s it was the end of an era; no passenger trains stop here now and the station is a goods yard for one of the local industries. I think maybe there's a few folks in high places who wish the railways were back now that the roads are so congested!

It's been fun to reminisce. Hope to meet up again soon.

Love, M

PS. I have just arrived home to find that my friend, with whom I often share a G & T at lunchtime, has written to me about her own experience of London. It's quite a different perspective because she was born there, worked, and commuted daily when she moved to Sussex.

Here's an extract from her letter:

> *My first recollection of London trains is going, with my parents, to Euston for our bi-annual trip to Glasgow Central, where we visited my grandparents. Dad and I always went to look at the steam engine. He enjoyed the experience more than me, but the recollection brings a smile to my face.*
>
> *Until I moved to Sussex in 1991, I always travelled to work by tube. In fact tubes were very much part of my working and social life. The worst thing about them is the rush hour, because one never knows who one is going to be pressed against; there is no choice unfortunately!*

My tube journey to the office was from one end of the Metropolitan line to the other. There were two advantages to this; I always got a seat, and if I fell asleep, someone would always wake me up at the last stop. I'm sure it was my imagination that saw regret on their faces, when they realised Uxbridge or Aldgate East was my actual stop! Sleep was unavoidable sometimes, of course, given an early start to the day or a busy lunchtime meeting at the local wine bar.

My friend and I, when we were ten (1948), joined a club for children at the Natural History Museum and travelled from Alperton to South Kensington on our own. Imagine that happening today! We had talks there, were shown all manner of interesting things and were allowed to sit and paint some of the exhibits. The highlight, however, was getting on the Hounslow train on the way home, instead of the Uxbridge one, so that we had to go back to Acton Town and get the right train. We thought this was great fun!

I think that our early experiences of travelling by train, although very different, show that we enjoyed them in different ways.

M

LETTER 11.

27th August 2007

Dear B

More on steam trains!

BJ and I have just returned from our holiday in the West Country, and while there we travelled from Dunster Beach, where we were staying, to Minehead on the steam train. The station had changed little. The old ticket office is the same and on the platform there is an old luggage trolley piled high with old trunks and leather suitcases. The porters used to load them and when the train arrived put the entire luggage in the guard's van.

We chugged along the line past the level crossing, which used to have a gate and a railway cottage next to it. When I was a child the gatekeeper was called Cornelius and his wife Honeysuckle; we used to make a point of walking to see them each year from the beach where we stayed on holiday even if we were not travelling by train. I think the names fascinated and amused us and we so enjoyed listening to their strong West Country dialect.

On our return to Dunster station after a great day at the seaside, I thanked the porter who appeared to be the same one that sold us the train tickets. I told him what an enjoyable trip it had been. He said, "Oh, that wasn't me here this morning it was my twin brother, but I'm glad you had a good day." They were identical twins and he didn't seem bothered about my mistake; I guess it happens to them all the time.

It's now possible to have a day's course in how to drive the train, and there are longer courses for enthusiasts on railway and train maintenance – perhaps one day I will sign up for one – sounds like fun to me.

See you soon.

Love, M

LETTER 12.

18th November 2007

Dear B

I am on the early train today. I managed to find a space to park on the road near the station so no parking charges. That's a good start to the day.

Arriving on the station platform (it's cold this morning, just 3.5 °C on the car's temperature gauge as I drove along), I collected the usual free *Metro* newspaper and felt sorry for the girl standing on the corner, giving them out in the north-east wind, but she is bright and cheery.

On the platform a large, officious security guy wanted to see my ticket but since I hadn't yet bought it from the machine that was not possible. He looked at me suspiciously and watched me buy my ticket. It's a good job I'm not the nervous type, and I refrained from making any comment, but I thought: My dear fellow, do I really look like a criminal about to cheat the railway?

A train arrived almost straight away, to my delight. I was expecting to wait until 7.30 for the train to Victoria but the one that pulled into the station is going to London Bridge so I jumped on that without a second thought. I then spent five minutes searching for London Bridge on the underground map to see how to get to Earl's Court. I discovered it's a bit further than from Victoria. I have to take the Jubilee line to Westminster and then the District line to Earl's Court. A short walk should take me to my destination in Redcliffe Gardens, so I am glad it's sunny and my ankle is better!

A lady got on at the next stop and is very chatty. She informs me that she is getting off at East Croydon but is doing some work at a school in Brighton and visiting two aunts at the same time. She lives in Norwich and wouldn't like to live down here. I didn't really want to know – why do people tell me their life story in five minutes? She is not wearing a ring so is either single or divorced or widowed or maybe doesn't want to wear one. Doesn't matter really, I just noticed it.

My 'lady' doesn't talk now because some more people have arrived in the carriage and are finding the *Metro* paper interesting, so I have decided to write this letter. The new arrivals look very business-like in suits, and with varying degrees of baldness. Even if they weren't bald they tried to be by having number one haircuts.

I didn't find anything much in the *Metro* today, but maybe I didn't read it three times and I'm not interested in football or the collapse of Northern Rock. It's interesting, though, that the government are bailing them out and guaranteeing payment for all savers and investors in the bank. I do find Alistair Darling, the new chancellor, interesting with those dark eyebrows and white hair; they don't match, for goodness' sake! I can't imagine a woman not having the same colour for eyebrows and hair, but then maybe we could be trendsetters! What do you think?

The train arrived on time at London Bridge, but that there is no equivalent coffee bar to Bonapartes at Victoria is immediately obvious, so I made my way to the underground. Here I managed to get on a train to Monument where I changed for Earl's Court.

I managed to find the right place, having crossed Old Brompton Road, and stopped at a comfortable little café for an 'Americano' and a croissant, and felt much better.

It was quite tricky finding the house I wanted. It was a very long street with odd numbers along one side and even numbers on the opposite side. Of course I am on the wrong side of the road – odd numbers instead of even – so I walked right past my destination.

Crossing the road, I found it easily enough but it is a huge house divided into flats. Ah! There is a choice of bells to ring. What to dooo? I could ring them all and see what happens? Wait a minute, on closer inspection I can see that there is a bell for the office at the bottom of the column so I rang that. I hate intercoms – for some reason I always want to run away because I am afraid I might not know what to say and mumble unintelligibly in reply. A voice came over the intercom: "Yes, can I help you?" I say who I am, and am invited to enter through the front door, which immediately makes a horrible grating noise. I have been instructed by the voice to go down the stairs to the basement. The door opens easily so the grating noise must have done something. Inside, it is dark and I am in a dingy hallway and the door slams shut behind me. Help, this is a bit scary!

Fortunately, the stairs to the basement are under the main stairs, which I suppose makes sense if you think about it. The stairs, like all stairs to basements, in my experience, are narrow and twist down sharply. These are no exception. There is a handrail; so I put my handbag and briefcase in the other hand to hold on for support. I am still a bit anxious about my ankle which is aching. It's only two weeks since I sprained it. At every turn in the stairs, however, the handrail changes sides, so I have to change hands each time. Quite awkward! I expect 'the voice' who bade me enter is wondering why it is taking me so long to descend, to what seems like the bowels of the earth (well, the house anyway).

At last I find a person in the dingy office at the bottom. She introduces herself but it's an unusual, odd-sounding name, 'Ondi' or something similar, and I immediately forget what she said and didn't like to ask her to repeat it. She showed me into a sort of storeroom/playroom with lots of toys: rocking horse, teddy bear, etc. and children's pictures on the walls. It's dingy because there is little light, and the bulb has blown in the central light so the girl fixes it. I find out later that this is a mother/baby hostel so that accounts for my experiences here so far.

Apparently my student is on the way, so while I'm waiting I prepare lots of pages with appropriate headings and review the evidence needed for the unit. I enjoy a coffee which the woman with the unpronounceable name makes for me. Looking round the room, the only cheery thing is through the window where there is a garden. Apart from this it would be a dismal room indeed.

My student arrived and we managed to find enough evidence to complete the unit, so that makes it a satisfactory visit.

At lunchtime I set off for my next destination and easily found my way back to Earl's Court tube station, feeling rather hungry. Here, however, I managed to get on the wrong branch of the District line so had to get off at the next stop and cross the line to come back again. I changed lines and got on the Piccadilly line. I had a map with me and looked for a quicker route. So having transferred to the Hammersmith line at Hammersmith tube station by crossing the road, I alighted at Latimer Road and decided to catch a bus. No bus came, although there were people waiting, so I decided to walk and it is quicker than walking from Ladbroke Grove, where I usually get off, so that was great.

I had lunch, which the student had kindly saved for me, and although the office is busy and there were many interruptions, we managed to finish the final unit. At least I will finish writing it up tomorrow.

I caught the good ole No. 52 bus back to Victoria and was able to relax, enjoy the sights of London and reflect on all the visits we have made here which have been such fun.

At Victoria the fast Brighton train is waiting so I caught that, having wandered round trying to find platform 12, a bit like Harry Potter's 11¾ or whatever it is. It's a different platform from the usual ones for trains south to Brighton. The train is quite full, but I managed to find a seat and, fortunately, the trolley service starts at the back of the train so I am able to get a much-needed drink (water!) and a sandwich. (For once I resisted buying chocolate. I hope you're impressed!)

The rail company has improved the announcements over the tannoy for making sure you are in the right half of the train, by telling you the numbers of the coach. This is then confirmed once you are sitting on-board. That's great. In the past, I have often found myself sitting in the wrong half and had to move through a moving train, swaying and falling into people.

I hope there will be no more hiccups today as I am rather tired, but no doubt you will hear about it if there are!

It's been fun to come to London again – it is stimulating and interesting despite the unexpected.

Love, M

LETTER 13.

8th April 2008

Dear B

Here we go again. Hope you are still getting stronger today.

I'm on the train to Town with little stress so far, just a few near   hiccups.

At the station buying a ticket is another senior citizen trying to buy a ticket for London so I choose the other window because she seems to be taking a long time. However, the other ticket window only accepts cash today because the card machine or computer or something is down. So I have to wait at the first window anyway. I try to be very patient as this other senior citizen fills in a form for a new railcard because hers is out of date. The ticket seller fills it in for her, and on about the fourth attempt she manages to put her bank card in the right way round and tap in the pin at the right time so that it connects and she doesn't have to start all over again! By this time, I am getting fed up but at last it is my turn to buy a ticket. I have my bank card ready and say to the ticket seller, "This will be more straightforward," and hand her my senior railcard and ask for a day return to Victoria. She returns my card and says, "This is your bus pass," – so I am no brighter than the previous customer! How embarrassing! After some searching I find the right card and the transaction proceeds without further delay. I make a comment about senior moments to the ticket seller and she grins. I say that I hope her day will get better but she gloomily replies that she doubts if it will.

On the platform I buy a coffee and a sandwich from the cheery girl at the kiosk. Waiting with me on the platform is a man with a sort of long-haired Labrador dog with typically doleful eyes but its hair is much softer, and it is a very light sandy colour – so of course I make a fuss of it. For once I haven't got any dog biscuits with me to offer him.

Then along comes another passenger with a rucksack and two tall walking poles which I think is strange attire for a visit to the city, but I guess you can hike across London if you really want to.

The train is quite full which is unusual for this time of day, and it's only Wednesday. Opposite me is a coffee-coloured guy (not sure if I can say that, is it PC?) in his late teens with bandana and baseball cap; worn backwards of course – cool! He is also trying to grow a moustache and goatee beard but these are rather fine, so I am surprised when he answers his mobile to hear his deep, rich bass voice!

Sitting typing this, I realise that all the gardening I did yesterday has taxed my back muscles somewhat despite the hot bath and G & T afterwards.

Well, it's not raining, but I have my anorak just in case – I am thinking about you and hoping you are recovering from your cold which is taking a while to clear. I am encouraged by your text that you have slept well and are still a zombie!

Later.... Oh no, a delay!

The train is now going to Redhill due to problems at London Bridge and we are now sitting, not moving, waiting for an available platform at Redhill. And we've still got to go to East Croydon. The train is full, and for some reason the tannoy is very faint but I think the train manager is trying to say standard passengers can sit in first-class compartments – I wonder if that applies to senior citizens too. Maybe I'll just stay put.

The young guy with the bandana is getting fed up, he has his baseball cap all askew and keeps yawning. His iPod music must be sending him to sleep. It's now 11.00 a.m., and we should be at Victoria, looks like a fun day!

I am surrounded by foreigners, I could be abroad; two German-speaking people opposite and some unknown Middle Eastern language next to me. I'm English. Get me out of here!

Looks like it's gonna be a long journey so I think I will eat my cheese sandwich – I feel hungry suddenly! This proved to be quite difficult in a confined space and I manage to drop cheese bits everywhere; I think my travelling companions were not very impressed. But I don't care much; they will just have to come to the conclusion that the English are messy eaters.

Finally, we arrived at Victoria 30 minutes late but the rain, which started further back down the track, had fortunately stopped. The rest of the day was relatively uneventful but I was glad to catch the train at 4.15 without any further hitches. Rain again, as I travel home. It's been rather a gloomy end to the day so I shall write about a more exciting event.

Love, M

LETTER 14.

20th June 2008

Dear B

BJ and I have just come back from a holiday in Austria. We travelled by Eurostar on one of the Great Rail Journeys.

BJ's mum came with us and we met at Euston. The train manager was there to meet us, show us on board and assist with the luggage. We settled into our seats and began to take in our surroundings and fellow travellers.

We arrived at Cologne to spend the night before travelling on to Austria. This was an experience in itself because we stayed at a hotel right by the station. Arriving in the room, there were complimentary ear plugs on the pillow! Well, I guess you might expect something like that on a Great Rail Journey where presumably the assumption is that not everyone on board is a rail enthusiast and wants to go off to sleep to the sounds of trains coming and going. It felt like we were sleeping on the platform. Anyway, it proved not to be too bad and we had a reasonable night's sleep before continuing our journey to Jenbach in Austria.

Next day we boarded the train early, and it was a trip that took all day and didn't have the comforts of Eurostar. The train was fairly comfortable although the restaurant car was at the other end of the train. So I decided that the quickest way to get there was to run along the platform when the train stopped at the next station and dash into the restaurant car for something to eat and drink. (The more experienced of our travelling companions had brought a picnic.) It seemed I was not the only one with this idea because there was quite a queue and so the train had set off again before I had even got to the counter. I had to weave my way back to our carriage, swaying with the train and trying not to send the coffee and other purchases into an unsuspecting person's lap en route.

At two stations the train changed lines and we seemed to be travelling in the opposite direction! It was on this leg of the journey that I felt inspired to write a verse or two about our adventures. I will find a copy and attach it for you. Hope you don't think it's too naff!

Thanks for your text. So glad you are out and about today, which suggests you are on the mend?

Love, M

THE COLOGNE TO JENBACH EXPRESS!

Standing on the platform, waiting for the train,
Loading in the luggage, here we go again.
David's at the ready, Iain's got the map,
Everybody get on board; be careful, mind the gap.

Sit down in your seats, folks (some have got a table),
Crosswords, books and newspapers make us comfortable.
Ewan's got his camera – there's quite a lot to see,
Gazing out the window at the scenery.

We're flying through the countryside beside the river Reine,
Some folks are asleeping – it helps to pass the time.
The countryside is beautiful; vines all along the way
Ready for the harvesting; we'll taste the wine someday.

Past another station; I think the name is Worm,
But the way that we pronounce it makes the natives squirm,
So someone who knows better says it should be said as 'Varm',
And if we can remember that we shall not come to harm.

The next main stop is Stuttgart, and although it's rather brief,
We run along the platform where much to our relief,
The restaurant car is open and we can buy a snack,
Then stumbling and swaying, we eventually get back.

Now travelling past Ulm, Jeanne gives a sudden shout,
"That's the tallest spire you'll see today, if you will just look out,
And that's the river Danube." (On Geography she's hot.)
Iain grabs his camera to take another shot.

Margaret keeps on reading her book on the Queen Mum,
She might be lost without it and could be rather glum.
Ruth just sits quietly as the world goes rushing by,
She is just contented as on our way we fly.

"Which way are we going?" Peter cried out in despair,
"First it's this way; then it's that way. It really isn't fair.
We're changing our direction at Munich here again;
Am I facing to the front or backwards in this train?

"It happened back at Stuttgart in exactly the same way,
I really will be dizzy if this goes on all day."
Next comes a second engine to push up the hill,
Where quickly it decouples, and downward we quickly spill.

At just on three o'clock Derek comes up for a chat,
To give us all an update, about this and about that.
Then followed Gill as well and Irene with her bag,
"We're going out to get some air and I really need a fag."

Some folks were unhappy and disturbed by all the din
From some local natives; it really is a sin.
But don't be too upset by them, soon it will all cease,
Only one hour to Jenbach and then there will be peace!

21st July 2008

Dear B

On the train to London as usual to visit students!

Although this is a new sheet, my laptop still thinks I am in France, and so shows up nearly every word as a spelling error.

The day started well enough. I was up in time to have breakfast and called at the 'hole in the wall' in Shoreham for some cash. Here I asked for a mini statement which promptly blew away in the breeze just as the money was about to appear. Dilemma! – Cash or statement? Looking around quickly, I stepped on the statement to hold it down and leapt back to the machine to grab the cash. Fortunately no one is around to steal my money. I then dropped the statement again just as I was getting in the car, and had to chase it down the street!

Next I arrived at the station, having found my usual free parking space.

At the ticket office window I had my bank card and railcard at the ready. I asked for two tickets for London, one for today and one for tomorrow because I will be in London two days running. The girl behind the counter reminded me that I could not travel before 9 a.m. on the cheap rate. I said, "OK," knowing that I always catch the 8.44 to London and there has never been a problem; but I chose not to argue.

I looked at the tickets, having made the transaction, to discover that I had been issued with two day return tickets for Worthing. I said to the ticket seller that this is a mistake – I wanted two tickets for London. She looked at me in surprise and said I had asked for tickets to Worthing – why would I do that for goodness' sake? Did I have a senior moment or did the ticket seller?

Anyway, she reissued me the right tickets, cancelled the previous ones and gave me a refund. Hey ho, these things happen. It is the same girl that served me when I tried to buy a train ticket with my bus pass. Hope she didn't remember.

I trotted over to the other platform via the subway, noting that the steps had been painted so that you can see them more clearly. They have been painting the railings too, and the station looks quite charming in the sunlight with fresh green and cream paint and the buddleia out.

I bought a cup of coffee as I usually do at the little kiosk. The girl asked me how my daughter is and automatically poured me a cup of tea before I had time to ask for coffee.

Oh dear, mistaken identity again – it often happens that I seem to remind people of someone else – must have a universal face. I explained that I didn't have a daughter and would like coffee. Unperturbed she said she would drink the tea herself and gave me a coffee. She remembered me more accurately when I asked for just a half spoonful of sugar. This always makes her laugh because she cannot believe that it makes any difference. (But it does!)

Although it's sunny, it's a bit chilly so I am wearing my cardigan but the sleeves are too long and I have to keep pushing them up my arms or turn the cuffs back, which is even more 'aggy'.

The train is on time and I manage to get a seat in the first carriage with a table for my laptop (which as you know is very important!). Unfortunately, I am travelling backwards and on the off side of the train where the sun reflects off the screen, and I often cannot see a thing on it. I have to hum to myself until a cloud comes over or we round a bend or enter a tunnel! It also means that I will not have to walk so far at Victoria. Today I will be catching the No. 11 bus and Ed has told me that it is quicker to go out of Victoria via the side entrance which cuts off a corner. He knows the route because it is the one he takes on hospital visits.

I am now too hot, so take off my cardigan and stuff it in my rucksack. I find a rucksack so much easier in London; it gives you two free hands. Some things are in my pocket, like my mobile, and these trousers are great because they have pockets halfway down the legs so I can put things like my memory stick in.

The three people around me today are all guys who just do their own thing – one is reading a book; I can't see which one but he's very absorbed in it. The guy opposite has been on his mobile and has a gentle voice, but he mainly just gazes out of the window, deep in thought. The third guy across from me is reading a newspaper and wearing sunglasses so is equally non-communicative. The whole carriage is quiet – no one is talking, just the occasional chatter of a young child who is told to "Shhhhh." Perhaps everyone is tired after exciting weekends or just plain bored by travel.

This reminded me of last summer when BJ's family visited from New Zealand. The two children aged four and six had never been on a train. (In New Zealand everyone travels by road; these are the straightest I have met anywhere. Trains are limited mainly to freight trains carrying goods from North Island to South Island and vice versa. Freight trains even have priority over passenger trains!)

We decided to take the children on a short journey from Shoreham-by-Sea (our nearest station) to Littlehampton. When you arrive at Shoreham station it's necessary to walk across the line at the crossing in order to reach the ticket office. This in itself is an adventure, and left both children wide-eyed and open-mouthed as the barriers came down with the accompanying warning sound of an approaching train. The first train didn't stop at Shoreham and so sped past within a couple of feet of where we were standing. This was followed by a second train that was slowing up to stop at the adjacent platform.

Crossing the line was the second awe-inspiring event, trying not to step on the rails, which is quite difficult for very small feet.

The next experience of buying tickets and waiting on the platform proved to be equally exciting, with announcements over the tannoy of the next train (not ours) which pulled in beside us. It is fascinating for the children to watch people getting on and off and the stationmaster waving the train off with his red baton (ah, gone are the days of green flags and whistles; burly guards and porters with luggage trolleys). When the train had gone we moved forward carefully towards the edge of the platform, keeping well behind the now yellow lines (they were white once, weren't they? or non-existent) so that we could look up the line and see the red light and the signal. We watched the signal change to green and stood well back, hands tightly held while our train pulled in.

Finding a seat so that we could look out of the window is essential, and as the train started, the children's faces were still wide-eyed and they were often literally open-mouthed in amazement, especially when we went by a signal which dropped as we went by.

We stopped at each station, and had to answer questions about "Where are we?" "Do we get off now?" And "How much longer will we be on the train?" I think they were both excited and slightly scared at the same time. We arrived at

Littlehampton and had lunch by the sea before taking the train back to Shoreham with two tired but happy children.

Now we are at East Croydon – there is some basic graffiti painted on the walls – it really is quite clever as an art form but I guess in the wrong place – or is it? Isn't that the idea of graffiti artists, to cheer up gloomy places?

There's standing room only on the train now and only Clapham Junction to go before Victoria. I cannot imagine travelling by train (or bus, for that matter) in any other country where the natives don't talk to each other.

Return Journey:

Unfortunately, I missed the 3.15 train so have decided to catch the fast Brighton train. Well, it seemed like a good idea until two extra stops were put in!

The first at Three Bridges for people connecting to Southampton – that train is cancelled.

The second at Haywards Heath, where I got off the train. This unscheduled stop is because some children who should have got off at Three Bridges stayed on the train. How on earth do you manage to leave your kids on the train, for goodness' sake?!

Thinking about that though, I remember being left behind once at the seaside in Devon when I was about five years old. We had been watching the Morris Dancers on the prom and I must have been so entranced by the swirling handkerchiefs, jingling bells on the legs and the altogether jolly, colourful spectacle that I didn't realise I was alone and the whole extended family of aunts, uncles, cousins as well as brother, sisters, Mum and Dad had become bored or hungry and moved on. To my consternation on turning round, there was no one there. I don't know how but I ended up in a Lost Property hut on the seafront, perched on a very high stool, eating an ice cream that someone had bought to soothe a distressed child! Eventually someone decided I was missing, and all the grown-ups had assumed I was with another member of the party.

Well, I don't think there has been any permanent psychological damage, but perhaps it explains why I still get lost around towns and cities that I visit (or does it?) but don't feel scared because I know that eventually I will be found or find my way.

I don't think there are Lost Property offices for children anymore, but I have seen people in brightly coloured jackets on crowded Brighton beach with a sign on a tall pole saying Lost Children, or did I dream that as a good idea?

I will now catch the next train to Shoreham-by-Sea which is the one scheduled train from Victoria that I could have caught anyway, and get in at the same time: 3.45! So much for trying to take short cuts on train journeys!

Hope you have had a good day.

Love, M

LETTER 16.

5th August 2008

Dear B

Here we go again to London!

No prob in getting to the station, except on the way I remembered I needed a new senior railcard for the year, it ran out on 31st July. Not to worry, I thought, I have time to get a new one. I explained to the ticket seller, who looked for a form but he didn't have one. He suggested I look in the rack of leaflets behind me. I picked up what I thought was the right form, and just as I was about to fill it in (fortunately I had a pen in my pocket), the ticket seller said, "No, that's not the right one," and went to look in the back for another one.

Oh dear – there were none on the station so he would have to order some. He is very kind and gave me a new card, which I had to pay for of course, £20, and said I could fill in a form another day. Well, maybe I will remember one of these days!

The train is on time and I manage to get a seat in the first carriage with a table for my laptop (which as you know is very important!). I have remembered to sit on the far side of the train so the sun is not in my eyes; but as the sun is not shining, it doesn't really matter today anyway!

The guy opposite has a very large briefcase plonked on top of the table so there is no room for my laptop. I asked him to move it (ever so politely), and he managed to give me six inches of space – I didn't have the courage to ask for more room or suggest he put it in the luggage rack overhead. He looked very important, and would probably have been better off in a first-class carriage.

At the next stop, Hove, two women and a man got on and it took them ages to decide who is going to sit by who because there were not three seats together. The man of course had the final say, and I drew the short straw because this very large guy then sat down by me, and took up a seat and a half. So I am a bit hemmed in – what with the briefcase and all.

The last seat is occupied by a bored-looking businessman who promptly fell asleep with his mouth open; I was so tempted to flick something in and look busy, but I refrained and got on with some work.

At Victoria I needed to go to the loo despite the now exorbitant cost of 30p. Fortunately, I had the right change and hastily put the two coins, 20p and 10p pieces respectively, in the slot, but they managed to get stuck so the turnstile wouldn't go round. I could see the coins were stuck by peering in the slot, so I had the bright idea of trying to push them further in with a 2p bit. At which point an elderlyish gentleman with funny crooked teeth (or is he really smiling?) looked at me kinda sadly and said that I needed more than two pence. I patiently explained that my money was stuck, and he thought I might be able to get in anyway. Are you kidding? I thought, but tried to push the turnstile to keep him happy and of course it was not possible. He also suggested I push the money return button, which I did to keep him happy; although I had also done that. It doesn't give you your money back if it's stuck, does it? Obvious really.

Finally I saw a guy in a bright, luminous jacket and I asked him to help me out of my predicament which is now getting rather urgent. He immediately produced a screwdriver and waggled it in the hole. And hey presto! The money is refunded! The guy put the money in for me, perhaps to show me how, and I am able to go in. (Maybe I should carry a screwdriver in my handbag in future for such emergencies, or would it be considered an offensive weapon if I was stopped and searched by the police?)

There is a long queue in the loo which you don't expect when you have to pay 30p. So I sat on the loo for a long time to write this up in my notebook and have my money's worth.

Even the water is rationed when you put your hands under the automatic tap, and to deter you doing it twice, the water is very hot. I used loads of tissues to dry my hands – more value for money.

I am back on the No. 52 today to Ladbroke Grove, and there is a traffic diversion because there are major building works at Knightsbridge, but no matter, I get an extra bit of a ride. The bus is modern with an automatic tannoy telling you what the stops are – I could have done with that the first time I went to Ladbroke Grove. I also noticed lots of bendy buses still. I expect Boris J has more important mayoral duties at the moment than getting rid of them – like seeing his barber on a regular basis.

The rest of the day goes without any unforeseen incidents so I enjoy the day, and the sun is now shining to cause me problems on the screen on the way home in the train, typing this up. One day I will get the perfect seat and companions – maybe...

Love, M

PS. Helen has been relating some of her commuting experiences, by train on the same route as me. Here's an extract from her recent letter:

The excitement when moving to Sussex was to travel by a 'proper train'. I quickly joined one of the groups who met at Shoreham station – same group, same train, same spot on the platform, every day. We were rather noisy, and did the Telegraph crossword. People sometimes moved seats to escape our chatter; it was not acceptable to all first thing in the morning! The most awful thing was getting on and finding someone sitting in 'our seats'. These part-time travellers have no conscience when they just sit anywhere!

The evening group was more assorted, as we sometimes worked late, but we always sat in the same seats, gossiping, and laughing, as we recounted tales of the events of the day.

One of the regulars commuting with her was christened 'No Socks' because he never wore any. Perhaps he had sweaty feet or something. He used to tell jokes. Here is one of the more successful ones: What is the quickest way to a man's heart? Answer: A knife in the back! I don't know if they found that amusing, but Helen recounted it at the office that day to her colleague, Jinx. He thought it a great joke and sent it in to the Financial Times (I thought this was a serious newspaper!), and he won a bottle of whiskey. Helen recounted this to her friends on the train, and this stimulated No Socks to think of even more jokes, but none of these subsequent ones was successful in winning a reward.

I think I will have to be more observant of fellow passengers and which seats they are heading for, so that I don't upset the system of the regular commuters, or maybe I should sit near them to share the jokes!

15th September 2008

Dear B

I think our day out to Buckingham Palace is one of the most exciting and enjoyable visits to London, although you were not well after a bad cold.

The journey to Victoria was uneventful, despite my insistence at Shoreham station that we walk right to the far end of the platform so that we could get into the first carriage and there would not be so far to walk at Victoria. This is my habit whenever I catch the early train. It turned out that this later train at mid morning is only four carriages long, so when the train pulled in we had to scurry back along the platform because it stopped only halfway along. So much for being a 'Noddy Know All!'

I had already sussed out how far it is to walk to the Palace from Victoria and how long it would take us. It was just as well that I did, because I took a wrong turn and instead of turning left crossed the road and found myself in a small garden. What is it about my sense of direction in towns and cities? I have no sense of direction and am easily disorientated (although I can find my way halfway across the world to the USA). I asked some workmen who were having a tea break the way to the Palace and they pointed me in the right direction.

I found the signposts difficult to follow with all the traffic and lights and people. (Well, that's my excuse anyway!) Today there is no problem, and once off the train we found our way easily and it is only a five-minute walk! We had our printout from the internet for our pre-booked time at midday and eventually found the entrance and bought souvenir programmes, as you do. There is little queuing to get in and the palace staff were well spoken and very helpful.

We were given headsets with a commentary for each room. This proved to have several advantages: firstly, that everyone is listening to the commentary so we moved round the Palace quietly, and secondly, that the information is clear and about the right length. It gave you some options for further information and took you from one room to another smoothly.

There were guides in each room and when we asked a question they were all very knowledgeable.

BJ remembers the displays of royal gifts from around the world so carefully selected and displayed with some contemporary and recent gifts and some inherited from previous generations. The art gallery is impressive and the commentary on the selected paintings left me wanting to know more about the artists and also the other paintings. We also had an insight into the behind the scenes preparations for a state banquet from the laying of tables, decisions on the menu to the timing of each course and final presentation of each course.

I agree with BJ that the Palace, although grand and opulent, has a very homely feel to it.

We could not take photographs until we were outside again on the steps at the back of the Palace. I sat on the steps while you took the camera to take photos of me and BJ. I was promptly asked by one of the palace staff not to sit on the steps. Quite right on reflection; it probably looked untidy and prevented the other visitors behind us moving off the steps.

It is such an advantage having a digital camera because not only can you select the pictures you want but also delete the less successful, like the first one you took of BJ and me and managed to cut our heads off. The second is a good one. Well done!

On the way out we went into the souvenir shop. This, again, is a delight with so much variety and good quality things to buy and at a range of prices. BJ and I decided it would be a good idea to buy souvenirs as Christmas presents to send to the family in New Zealand. We later parcelled them up and sent them off, and they were a great success.

As we walked out past the great lawn and through the grounds, I pointed out a heron by the lake through the trees but you were convinced (I think) that it was a model. It was so still. As we argued about this one, we asked one of the guides who said, "Ladies, please," and in a witty, light-hearted way assured us it was in fact a real heron. So I was right after all!

By now we were starving, and we came out onto a different road so had no idea where we were. Fortunately, BJ has a better sense of direction than me and we turned left and headed back to Victoria. The first restaurant we came to was The Mango Tree and since there were no others in view we went in. It is a Thai restaurant and it is expensive but I guess not by London standards, especially in Belgravia, and we all agreed it was a special day out and we would treat ourselves. Inside the restaurant it is spacious and had soft lighting with a Thailand-like feel. We were greeted at the door and the hospitality of the staff made us feel special.

Later we found out that The Mango Tree is a highly renowned Thai restaurant and is part of a parent company, Coca, in Asia. The Mango Tree became the flagship Thai restaurant in Europe, and has won awards commending their food creations and polished service. It is feng shui designed to enhance the dining experience. And winner of the Thai Chef of the Year 2003 award in the Fusion category. The Mango Tree offers 'innovative yet classic cuisine of the highest calibre'. Using the very finest ingredients sourced from the best suppliers, both locally and abroad, the restaurant serves genuine Thai dishes from each of the four main culinary regions: rich and mild dishes from the North, spicy food from the East, mild food influenced by the Chinese cooking style from the Central region, and hot and spicy food from the South.

We could choose from dishes such as Pla Pow, a grilled fillet of sea bass wrapped in banana leaf and fresh lemon grass served with spicy lime sauce, Larb Pla Tuna, a north-eastern-style tuna salad with dry chilli and lemon grass or Gaeng Kiew Wan Gai, corn-fed chicken in green curry.

We arrived home tired but with very happy memories of our day out. It is such a change for me to have a leisurely day out without any work commitments and not having to carry a laptop.

Love, M

LETTER 18.

14th October 2008

Dear B

On the way to London again.

Nothing unusual so far about the journey today, but then the train has not yet reached Haywards Heath, so plenty of time for adventures and the unexpected!

At the station I bought a sandwich, and the guy at the counter still thinks I come from Barnham and that I usually wear a uniform! I would like to meet this 'double'.

I wonder what he says when she buys her cheese sandwich or asks why she isn't in uniform. (I don't know what uniform; perhaps I will ask him next time.) I wonder where she goes or has come from – intriguing.

I have bought my usual coffee from the cheerful girl at the kiosk and today added some chewing gum as well. I need that to concentrate and wake my brain up while walking through London. There is an article about the beneficial effects of chewing gum in the paper, so it must be right! It helps stimulate muscles and blood supply to the brain or something.

I suggested the kiosk girl have a pot for tips and she said that other folks had suggested that as well. She might get one. I felt a bit mean after that because I didn't leave a tip – well, there isn't a pot to put it in....

It's quite a mild sunny day, and as usual there are several suited businessmen on the platform, waiting at the far end so that they can get on the front of the train where there is a first-class compartment. This always seems to me a bit pointless because there are so few seats and more often than not someone sits there after the train manager has checked the tickets and gone back down the train to his little office with the high stool. That's if he can get through in the first place after East Croydon where loads of folks get on.

Anyway these two 'gentlemen' chat to each other but don't acknowledge anyone else, and are obviously of public school background. Their conversation today is about the economy and general doom and gloom despite Gordon Brown's rescue package for the banks.

The usual announcements over the tannoy tell travellers that they cannot take their bikes on the train between 7 a.m. and 10 a.m. on trains into London and trains into Brighton.

Strange really, because that's just when people are going to work and being environmentally friendly. Maybe I will write to the train companies and point that out and suggest an extra carriage (specially adapted, of course) be added for cyclists. Maybe I won't. The guard's vans on old trains used to have a special compartment for bikes and large goods like my college trunk. I guess these are no longer in service due to economic pressures!

The other tannoy announcement, as always, is about not leaving luggage unattended and that if you do it will be removed and destroyed. I wonder how many times this has happened to innocent passengers who have gone to buy a coffee or newspaper from the kiosk. The announcement also says that if I see anything suspicious to report it. I have never seen anything suspicious yet, which is a bit boring. I think it would be exciting to find something 'suspicious' and report it. I think the laid-back station staff would be both surprised and probably not believe me. I mean, whoever would want to leave anything suspicious on the platform at Shoreham-by-Sea? Where would you leave anything suspicious? Even the litter bags are transparent so you can see everyone's rubbish! Perhaps it would be interesting to check the litter bags more closely next time I am waiting for a train. I could stand and wait next to one and surreptitiously observe the rubbish and, perhaps more importantly, who throws what in the bin. I don't think I'm cut out to be a sleuth.

At Gatwick Airport, as usual, travellers got on with large cases and had nowhere to put their luggage. It is amazing there are no luggage racks on this route – I feel another letter coming on to the rail companies on this line. This is such a convenient station for ongoing passengers who are arriving or departing from the airport; its position in the airport is excellent. I've used it several times for journeys overseas.

Not far to Victoria now we have just left Clapham Junction. I am always surprised that this is the busiest station in Europe. I looked it up once out of interest.

Apparently 2,000 trains pass through every day and it is a favourite place for train spotters (that's some task – 2,000 spots a day. You could probably see the whole lot in a short space of time! Do they keep records or take photographs or maybe both?). At the moment they're not very popular with the government and police because they may be seen as a terrorist threat on mainline stations!

Now we are passing Battersea Power Station, another interesting place. After all the effort put into constructing its four chimneys which spanned 25 years, probably due to the war years holding up progress, it was completed in 1955.

It managed to produce electricity until 1989 and is now derelict. It was made a grade II listed building in 1983 so can't be pulled down, but in spite of many ideas for its development and future use, nothing has happened yet. It looks a bit sad and neglected to me. I hope they come up with something soon.

As the train pulls into the platform at Victoria there are the usual three announcements from the train manager over the tannoy: "Mind the gap between the train and the platform."

I do find this a bit of a problem when I have a case with me. I have never been able to decide whether it's best to leap across the gap first and then reach for the case or hurl the suitcase off first and then jump off afterwards, but it's OK today, no problem. It's equally difficult, if not more so, to combat 'the gap' when you are catching the train.

"Take all your belongings with you." Well, I usually manage that, and have so far been fortunate in that nobody has stolen anything en route. I remember you telling me that your case was stolen once when you travelled to Scotland. That must have been awful for you.

"There will be a delay of thirty seconds before the doors open." This always seems like an eternity to many travellers, who can't wait, it seems, to press the yellow 'Open' button for the door and are eager to be the first to alight as though it was some competition. Even if you do manage to be first off, the chances are that you will be held up by the rush along the platform and the queue at the ticket barrier, which always operates at its own automated pace anyway. Today is no exception. I admire the 'old lags' who patiently wait in their seats for everyone else to scramble off before leaving the train in a much more dignified way and no doubt complete with all their 'belongings'.

Today I decided to take the side entrance out of Victoria station. My neighbour says it's quicker and you can catch more buses going down King's Road. I couldn't remember the number of the bus which I usually catch (senior moment!), it's two months since I've been to World's End after all and a lot has happened in two months!

Nonplussed, I left by the side entrance and unfortunately turned right instead of left and ended up on the wrong bus. I did ask the driver if he went along King's Road and he nodded. He was English so I knew he understood my question, and that this would definitely be the right bus. He didn't tell me that it turned off halfway down King's Road and when we turned into a side street I had to get off and walk back. It didn't really matter – it is a pleasant walk in the sunshine and along King's Road; it's quite interesting – starting with the expensive shops at the Sloane Square end and gradually getting cheaper towards World's End. Today there are several closing-down sales in the expensive shops – I guess the downturn in the economy is affecting them while the charity shops will have a boom time.

I had a good day at the Care Centre, although I didn't enjoy the bacon buttie I had on arrival – it was too fatty; and I did just fancy one. The lunch was lamb hotpot and I didn't fancy that. Later, I realised that was yesterday's menu and that really I could have enjoyed a chicken casserole today!

I have now remembered it's the No. 11 bus that goes up and down King's Road to Victoria so I have no problem finding it this time. The bus is unexpectedly crowded, and when the person next to me gets off another lady immediately moves to sit by me. She turns out to be an interesting character from Dublin. She explains that she has moved seats because the woman across the aisle in the red shoes (reading *Farmer's Weekly*) had refused to let her sit by her and just pointed to the disabled area. This Irish lady is understandably in high dudgeon about this. I chatted to her for a while and she tells me about the cost of renting flats in Chelsea – up to £2,000 a week! I don't think she lives in such palatial digs though. She is a dog walker and is off to collect a dog to walk in Hyde Park; this appears to be her way of getting some extra money in the capital and seems a good idea to me.

The journey home is good, and I am reading *The Boy in the Striped Pyjamas*. It's very interesting and thought provoking.

That's all.

Love, M

LETTER 19.

16th October 2008

Dear B

I have written two poems. The first describes the difficulties which might be encountered by a traveller arriving at Gatwick and wanting to catch the train to London or the South Coast as part of their onward journey.

The second one is about the possible frustrations of cyclists who are unaware of the train rules and times when you can take a bike on board for use when alighting at their destination.

What do you think? Should I send them to the railway companies? I think they're more interesting than complaining letters, but perhaps they wouldn't take any notice of them anyway.

Love, M

TRAVELLING BY TRAIN WITH A SUITCASE

Been thro' baggage and collected my cases,
Tripped over my shoes so tied up the laces,
Down to the platform to catch the next train,
Holding an umbrella to keep out of the rain.
No seats in the carriage, I sit at the back.
No room for the luggage in the overhead rack,

My case has to stand on its end on the floor,
And unfortunately blocks the train's closing door,

So I alight once again,
With my case in the rain,
And vow never again
To travel by train.

(Well, at least not with a case from the airport!)

CYCLING TO WORK

I've a new job in Brighton,
And need to get there by train,
But I have to get to the station,
In the fog, the sunshine or rain.

My bicycle's new and shiny,
I've oiled the wheels and the chain,
Adjusted the saddle and handlebars
And practised riding along the lane.

My helmet is blue and yellow,
With a strap fitting under the chin.
My rucksack is ready beside me,
I think I've put everything in.

Cycle clips secure my trousers,
And I've tucked them into my socks,
So they can't get caught on the pedals,
In the wheels, or in the brake blocks.

I've a spanner in my pocket,
So the bike can be folded in two,
And fit neatly into the carriage,
In the space right next to the loo.

I've already bought my ticket,
To save time having to queue,
When a voice comes over the tannoy
To say that the train is due,
AND
"Passengers are reminded that cycles
are not allowed on trains between 7 a.m. and 10 a.m."
Oh no! Whatever shall I do?
I can't take my bike on this train,
After all the preparing I've done.
My new job's waiting in Brighton
But I won't get there until one.
What a dilemma!
What a fuss!
I'll just have to travel on the very next bus.

LETTER 20.

21st January 2009

Dear B

Got your text. Thanks.

Yes, I am on the train to London; the first trip this year and it's already been quite interesting....

For a start I nearly got run over crossing the road to the station; a car at the junction didn't see me as I stepped off the kerb, but I am still in one piece although I think both parties were a little shocked and thought the other person an idiot.

I bought a sandwich for £2 at the station kiosk – cheese and pickle because that's the least squishy to put in my rucksack; anything with mayonnaise is very squishy and I don't fancy sausage and bacon – too greasy anyway.

At the ticket booth there were several people in front of me, and although two windows were open I hovered between the two to wait for the next available one. I expected a long wait. At one booth a guy was finding it difficult to get a through ticket to Stansted Airport but I'm not sure why.

At the other an elderly, well-heeled and well-spoken couple were asking loads of questions about how to buy tickets on the internet. The latter were obviously not commuters and in no hurry, and completely unaware of the queue behind them. The queue moves forward and the next woman wanted a complaints form. The poor ticket seller looked upset but the woman explained: "It isn't your fault, I'm fed up with paying ten per cent extra (the latest increase in ticket prices) and the train is always late." He gave her the relevant form and she marched off. I was next and smiled cheerily at the ticket seller and said, "This will be easier for you," and do you know what? For once it was straightforward!

I bought a cup of coffee from the cheery girl at the kiosk who gave me loads of coins in change because I only had a £10 note. This was a bit of a nuisance because my pockets are shallow in my coat, but I wrapped it all in a tissue so it would be safe.

On the platform was a burly policewoman, and I thought, gosh, she's a bit short – not much taller than me. Further observation showed that she was as broad as she was tall, mainly due to all the gear she has to carry (do they still have hidden truncheons or just CS gas?) and probably a bulletproof vest. I was certain that if she had to lean forward she would fall over from all the weight up front!

They had changed the large posters on the billboards; a smiling Moira Stewart reminding everyone to pay their income tax before the end of the month, and I felt quite smug because I have already, and had a rebate from overpayment last year.

On the other billboard was an advert for Virgin Atlantic and 'red hot fares', and I resolved to use my Virgin credit card more for purchases to boost up my air miles (currently standing at 56!).

I was taking all this in and making notes on my mobile when my train arrived and I scurried up the platform to get near the front. I managed to spill my coffee as I hurried along by squeezing the polystyrene mug too tightly and it sprayed all down my coat. Another dry-cleaning bill!

There had been several announcements over the tannoy about delayed trains from Havant, and eventually the reason given was that there was ice on the line. It's quite difficult to hear the tannoy announcements sometimes because they seem to stimulate the herring gulls, which are always present on the roof, to start a major screeching session. They were always a nuisance when I lived in Dover, especially in the mating season, but that can't be the reason today, because it's only January. (Unless they're starting earlier than usual!)

The train was quite crowded today and by Preston Park there was standing room only, but I had a seat and room for my laptop. It was hot on the train so I had calmly organised myself with my rucksack behind the seat and coat on my lap; coffee, mobile and ticket neatly to the right.

The woman next to me was writing frantically but her writing was very untidy and I couldn't see what it was about, so my curiosity is not satisfied but I think it was business related and therefore probably boring! (I found a way to type so that the person next to me or standing in the aisle can't read what I am writing, which is a good idea because it might be about them in a minute!) The 'scribe' then dropped her pen while answering her mobile, and I scrabble about under the seat to help her find it but it had rolled away under a fitted metal box so it's gone forever!

The rest of the compartment were a mixed bunch but all had the early morning bored look, gazing out the window, reading newspapers or sleeping and totally ignoring all fellow passengers.

All goes well with my student and I headed back to Victoria on the tube. Waiting to see which platform the train will depart from, I find myself next to two women who have been to London for the day but who have different destinations for their homes. One was heading for Lewes and one for Portslade; it proved to be extremely difficult to explain to these two friends that they can get on the same train but sit in different compartments. I tried saying as clearly as I could, "The front part goes to Littlehampton and the last four carriages to Eastbourne when the train divides at Haywards Heath."

Finally, they managed to understand and boarded the train. One friend followed me to the fourth carriage where she then had a long debate with herself on where to put her suitcase, after much 'umming' and 'aahing'. It ended up on the table in front of me so there was no hope of me using my laptop on the way home without further stress for my travelling companion. Just before the train departed she glanced at her ticket and gasped. It was the one for Lewes – her friend had given her the wrong one. So I looked after her suitcase while she walked swiftly back through the train to find her pal and swap tickets. Finally she was able to settle down after long explanations about her friend being a control freak and it might have been better for them to travel to Brighton and change trains there rather than wait so long on the station at Victoria. Oh well, I guess that could be an option.

I contented myself with reading the 'writing magazines', looking for tips on writing and ways to get on the editorial and publishing ladder.

Love, M

LETTER 21.

3rd February 2009

Dear B

Snow! Five inches of it we measured in the garden this morning, so I am writing to you from home when I should be on the train to London.

There are no trains – as usual the railways have been brought to a halt by the weather, despite the forecasts from the Met Office over the past few days which have been surprisingly accurate.

It's not even the wrong kind of snow, just too much of it. Well, that's according to Boris Johnson, the Mayor of London, and the 'wrong quantity', so it must be right. Whatever! It's paralysed the capital, bringing all train services from the south into London to a halt. So no trains to Victoria today.

No buses are running in London either, because they are apparently snowed up at the depots; the gritters not having cleared the entrances so they can get out.

No tube trains are running in the underground either. The city is still and comparatively quiet because there are not many taxis out and about so there is little traffic. The motorways into London are gridlocked too, both on the M25 and the M2 from Kent, which seems to have had the most snow.

What a joy for most of us to have an extra and unexpected day off – to walk in the snow, take wonderful photographs.

It would have been wonderful if we had travelled up yesterday and got stuck in London. We could have joined in the excitement of the children in Hyde Park having snowball fights and sledging. The more imaginative folks have apparently not only built traditional snowmen (with coal for eyes, a carrot for a nose and a smiley face) but also created snow bears, a man with his dog on a park bench and an attempt to build an igloo.

The more determined, or maybe desperate, workers have walked to work or even skied. One person training for a trek to the Arctic must have been delighted with the additional practice in the cold environment right on her doorstep.

Another traveller interviewed, who has just returned to Gatwick from a skiing holiday in Switzerland complete with skis, got off the plane and promptly got on them again to ski home! As usual there are different views on the weather and our ability to cope, but I love this weather. What An amazing winter wonderland for a whole day. It makes everyone pause, take stock, slow down and rearrange their plans.

I have called in on our elderly neighbours to check they are all right and not in need of anything. They are fine, their house is warm and they have enough food in the freezer to feed an army.

BJ, R and I are now off for a walk with the dogs in the fields and to take photographs.

It reminds me of our holiday in the mountains in Switzerland at Christmas last year. We (that's BJ and me) stayed in a hotel right in the centre of Kandersteg. It had snowed heavily and we were able to watch the skiers of varying degrees of expertise making their way to the cable car to ascend to the top.

Sledges were also popular and not only for children but for local people dragging their shopping home. I have no experience of skiing and although BJ tried it, with some success, in Vancouver several years ago she was not inclined to repeat the activity. It is still fun to watch everyone else having a go. We did try a night hike wearing snowshoes but this was quite tiring and we gave up after a few fields, but it was enough to give us a taste of the 'sport' and the enchantment of a winter's night.

We walked through the woods and part way up the mountain and of course took many photographs. The climbing wall in the children's playground had a spectacular sheet of ice covering it. We were not prepared for the icy pavements and deep snow which you had to walk through whenever you went out, so our priority was to invest in suitable footwear! I am wearing the very same boots today, so it was a good investment! I also invested in some expensive sunglasses because the glare of the snow made my eyes water, but I think these will be unnecessary today.

We took a journey by train from Kandersteg down to Oeschinensee and took a wrong turning trying to find the station entrance but eventually managed it. On the platform a very efficient 'snow blower' was sending the snow in great cascades onto a side line.

The train was on time and spotlessly clean; no graffiti anywhere! It was very comfortable and geared up for skiers with special racks in each carriage for skis. The train continues in the other direction up the mountain until altitude prevents it from going higher, and further transport is only by cable car.

The highlight of the holiday was a horse-drawn sleigh ride on Boxing Day. We went around the village streets and through the woods. It had an ingenious mechanism for crossing the road where the snow had been partly cleared. The sleigh runners could be lifted up and wheels lowered so that the horse could more easily cross. The reverse then happened as we came to deep snow where the wheels were raised and the sled runners lowered.

We also took a bus (yes, a bus) from the village down the steep mountain road to look at some frozen lakes and a trout farm. The roads were clear, and again like the train, the bus was on time – we missed the one coming back up the hill by one minute! We had to wait half an hour for the next one. Fortunately there was a little chalet café where we could keep warm and have a coffee. I guess if you have snowy, icy conditions for several months of the year then adapting for efficient travel becomes essential.

Later ... we have literally ploughed through the snow and almost wish we had snow shoes, like the ones we wore for the night hike in Kandersteg, or a sledge. BJ had the idea of harnessing the dogs to pull us along, but I don't think that would work; they would probably take off in the wrong direction or different ones with Bruno going one way and Max the other!

It's amazing what people can find in their sheds and garages to use as toboggans – even dustbin liners seemed to be quite effective today.

We are now back home and enjoying the last bottle of mulled wine left over from our New Year open house morning. It's been an exhilarating morning but I think some serious snow clearing is the next task, to clear the gateway and the drive!

Hope you enjoyed your day.

Love, M

PS. Thinking about difficulties of travelling in London today, I have written a few verses about all the possible ways of getting from one place to another across the city.

LONDON TRANSPORT

Now once again
I'm on the train,
Out of the rain,
On the way to London.
Now out in the air,
It's bright and fair,
I haven't a care,
Walking along in London.
Now hailing a cab
Which is rather 'fab'
(Despite a large tab),
Looking out on London.

Now in a rickshaw
Ringing bells; draw
Us; no comfort of straw,
Right across London.
Now on the bus
Without any fuss;
No need to rush
When crossing London.
Now underground
In the tube I'm found;
Great rumbling sound,
Hurtling below London.

Now on a horse
In Hyde Park of course,
An unusual resource
In some parts of London.
Now at the dock,
Taking a boat thro' the lock.
Time to take stock
On the Thames in London.
Now on a bike,
In for a hike
Pedalling; I dislike
Cycling through London.
There's nothing to lose
Whatever you choose;
There always are views
About the way to travel in London.

Hope you like it. I think it sums up most of the ways people travel around London, and we have tried some of them. Cycling and taking a rickshaw I don't think would appeal to either of us, although I'm sure the Mayor would approve – but you never know!

Hope to catch up with you soon.

M

LETTER 22.

24th February 2009

Dear B

Today I am travelling to London but for a different purpose: to spend a few days with my sister in Staffordshire. BJ dropped me off at the station in good time for the train.

On the way we could see at the end of one road some people wearing brightly coloured luminous yellow-green jackets standing on the pavement. We commented that there seemed to be rather a lot of them and wondered if there was some sort of demonstration going on. As we drove nearer, to our amazement it was a whole class of about 30 very young children accompanied by teachers, all wearing safety jackets complete with school logo. They were seen safely across the road in a long caterpillar; two by two and each child holding a lunch box. As I mounted the steps to catch the train, the brightly coloured 'human caterpillar' arrived on the platform, chattering with excitement and lined up against the wall for safety. Curiosity overcame me and I asked one of the accompanying adults, "Where are you going?" "To the toy museum in Brighton," was the reply. What fun! No wonder they were so excited. There is an amazing collection of toys there: puppets, toy soldiers, games, dolls, model trains and cars, to name but a few. It is located right outside the station underneath the arches, so there will be only a short distance to steer the 'caterpillar' once they arrive at Brighton.

I think it was a relief to other travellers waiting for trains that they got into the carriages of the next train which drew along the platform. I suspect the passengers already in the train had a shock, but it is only a ten-minute ride to Brighton to endure, or enjoy, the chattering class of children.

Sitting on the seat to wait for my train, I couldn't help but hear the conversation of the two women sitting beside me. (I mean, do I ever eavesdrop?) One was travelling to

Liverpool and said she would cross London by taxi. I pricked up my ears at this and, interrupting the conversation, I asked if I might share a taxi with her because that was my destination also. She was delighted to do this, and we chatted on and off on the way to Victoria to get to know each other a bit.

In the taxi my companion and I enjoyed the ride through London, taking in some of the famous sights and feeling quite grand as we were driven through Mayfair. Seeing the place names reminded me of the board game Monopoly which we used to play and which I think is probably still available. I remember Park Lane and Mayfair as the most expensive places to buy, and if you were fortunate to own them and build houses and hotels, it was possible to charge an exorbitant rent and rapidly bankrupt other players. Passing 'Go' always gave players a boost as they circumnavigated the board again – quite the reverse of a congestion charge. There were cards in the 'Community Chest' or 'Chance' piles which could trip you up with speeding fines, an unlikely event in London these days with the heavy traffic which still persists; the congestion charge in the inner city doesn't seem to have made a great deal of difference, does it? We still travel at the same average speed of a coach and horses.

There are cards for street repairs (perhaps these preceded the council tax!) which could make a hole in your bank balance, and unexpected rewards too as you moved round the board: £10 for winning a beauty contest; and a £200 bonus for a bank error in your favour! (I think this is probably a most unlikely event in the current economic climate, don't you?)

Our destination of Euston is not on the Monopoly board. I wonder who chose the four stations – Fenchurch Street I have never heard of. Where is that in London?

As we passed Pall Mall I remembered reading that there is a new statue of the Queen Mother which has recently been completed and unveiled by the Queen. It depicts her in her younger days, some distance from King George VI, which has caused some discussion on the appropriateness on both counts. I must go and see for myself next time I am in London.

I was glad that I had a companion on our arrival at Euston station because the taxi rank is below the station, down a slope. I think I would probably have turned the wrong way and got lost if I had been on my own!

I was feeling hungry by now so headed for a kiosk selling sandwiches and bought an egg and lettuce bagel clearly marked: 'No mayonnaise.' I always seem so dim when buying things on stations. I thought I was getting a bargain for £1.49 because the label said: 'Crisps and water for £1.49 with any sandwich.' Silly me! I thought that was for all three! But of course it's just the crisps and water in addition to the sandwich. Oh well, I just bought the sandwich and water, I didn't really fancy crisps.

The train was already in and was a Virgin train so as usual ordinary passengers like me have to walk past all the first-class carriages, which take up about half the train, before you can find a seat in second. It's often a good idea to reserve a seat on these northern-bound trains but there was no problem today. At peak times most of the seats can be reserved and often these are not filled. Sometimes I have sat in them anyway and rarely been turned out. I often have wondered why, perhaps folks have found another seat or missed the train.

Today I have found a seat just inside the compartment next to the luggage racks, at a table so I can use my laptop, with a socket to charge it (or your mobile phone). Excellent! Well done, Virgin trains! I am so glad to have my new laptop after the demise of the old one! This is what happened: I was leaving the house to visit a student in Horsham, briefcase in hand. As I came out the front door the post lady rode up on her bike to the gate with some letters, so to save her coming down the drive I went to collect them. She could see I was on the way out so opened the gate for me. I pushed the letters through the letter box in the front door, got in the car, started the engine and reversed out. There was an awful crunching noise because I had run over my laptop! I had put it down by the boot when greeting the post lady and forgotten I hadn't put it in the car! DISASTER! Inspecting the damage, I found that one side of the case was dented. Anyway, the outcome of this sad saga is that the house insurance covered the cost of a new laptop and the hard drive was rescued, so I fortunately didn't lose all my work and student records! I have written a poem about this escapade and will attach it for you to read.

Settling down in my seat, I started to eat my sandwich and this reminded me about an unpleasant incident once on the train back from Victoria. I was returning from a business trip to Macclesfield and had rushed across London by underground and was ravenously hungry. I just had time to buy a hot dog and coffee (how unhealthy is that!) before catching the very crowded commuter train to Shoreham.

I sat down in the only vacant seat I could find, but within two minutes, 'a man from the city' (I knew he had to be one of these because of the pinstriped suit, expensive-looking gold cufflinks and boring tie. No bowler hat though, I think these have maybe gone out of fashion because you don't see many of them in London these days. The proverbial black umbrellas are still in evidence come rain or shine and remind me of

James Bond and other thrillers where things are hidden in them or the spike turns into a gun or dagger.)

Anyway, this guy stood over me glowering and declared loudly, "That is my seat," just as I am about to take my first bite of the hot dog. What? I am rather taken aback as there was no seat reservation in evidence but he pointed to a briefcase, which apparently belongs to him, hidden in the space between the seats. The carriage was full and so I graciously stood up (well, as graciously as you can with a hot dog in one hand and a cup of coffee in the other!).

He, however, was not content as I have no option but to stand in the gangway next to him and continue munching my hot dog. He told me in no uncertain terms, "You should not be eating a hot dog on the train. You should only purchase food from the food bar on the train. People like you should not be allowed on the train eating food bought from a kiosk on the station." What planet are you on? I thought. I resisted pointing out that it's actually not possible to buy food on this train because there is no food bar and the train is so crowded that the trolley service can't get through. It only sells hot and cold drinks, crisps and shortbread anyway. Cheek! Why didn't he travel first class if he didn't want to be surrounded by plebs like me!

I decided not to rise to his bait and moved past a couple of folks to the end of the carriage to finish my hot dog. There I was cheered by sympathetic remarks from some workmen who had witnessed the whole debacle. The 'city gent' got off at East Croydon so I was able to have his seat anyway. Poor chap, maybe he had had a stressful day at the office. I felt sorry for his wife (if he has one) – hope she has his favourite meal ready tonight! Or maybe that's his problem, he doesn't like women.

Today all is well, and I can sit back, relax and enjoy my sandwich in peace.

Love, M

PS. I looked up information on Fenchurch Street station. It was the first station to be built in London and is the smallest. It's not far from the Tower of London and serves the line out to the East of London, through Tilbury to Shoeburyness in Essex. (Bet you really wanted to know that!)

M

LAPTOP CRUNCH

With bag in hand and briefcase too,
Laptop secure, knowing what to do
And where to go, I unlocked the car
When at the gate the postman came,
Not early or late, on time the same.
Through the letter box the letters went,
Only one for me which had been sent.
So off to Horsham, it's not far.
Start the engine, off I go.
Arrgh! There's a crunch from the wheels below.
As out of the gate I look back to see
What has happened? "Oh dearie me!"
My laptop and case lie there flattened.
How on earth can that have happened?
They are not in the boot as I supposed
But lying squashed there in the road.
Doom and Gloom descend on me
"But all is not lost," cries my friend B.
"The home insurance they will pay
So contact them without delay."
The drive's not broken, the story ends
Satisfactorily – thanks to friends.
The screen is shattered. The rest's intact,
All my work can be saved in fact,
Of which I am very glad indeed.
The lesson to learn I now must heed,
Put it all in the boot before you drive
Then there's no disaster when you arrive.

LETTER 23.

26th February 2009

Dear B

Just have to write to you today because I am on a train but not on the usual route to London.

I am staying with my sister and we are enjoying a day out on the Ffestiniog line to Portmadoc. So this train is pulled by a traditional steam engine, and we are sitting in a third-class carriage!

We only just made it on time. (I wonder where you have heard that before.) Setting off hopefully in good time, we missed a turning somewhere en route although we had downloaded the AA guidelines from the Internet. We pulled into a lay-by and retrieved the map from the boot to get us on track again.

It's a grey old day but the road through Snowdonia National Park is still beautiful, and one advantage of winter is that you can see further when the leaves aren't on the trees.

With ten minutes to go, we entered Ffestiniog scrutinising all the signposts for directions to the station, but there didn't appear to be any. We drove along the long winding street through the town and out the other side. To our relief, finally D spotted the sign off to the left and we arrived in the car park with two minutes to spare. Fortunately, the train was standing at the station and we rushed to get a parking ticket for the car, and for once I had sufficient coins for the machine. We ran down to the track and had no time to buy tickets, but the guard let us board the train because we assured him we could pay in cash during the journey.

So here we are, out of breath but have made it! The whistle blows, and with the typical huffing, puffing and clanking, the train pulls out of the station. Looking around, I can see the familiar windows (with a warning not to put your head out!)

and the red emergency chain with the threat of a £50 fine for misuse and the doors with the leather straps for opening the window.

This third-class carriage had red seats and small tables and was quite narrow, but there were only two other people as fellow travellers. We had no idea about how far it is to our destination or the time of the return train, but the other folks had an information leaflet which they kindly lent us.

There was a menu for snacks and drinks on the table, and soon a smart waiter, complete with bow tie, appeared to take our order. "I fancy a beer, an Old Speckled Hen," I said, and he wrote it down on his little pad.

While we waited for the drinks to arrive, I decided to explore the train and, swaying through the carriage, camera in hand, I made my way through the carriages to the front. It was a long train with about 15 coaches. To pass from one carriage to another, balancing on the footplates was quite a feat, requiring acrobatic balancing skills. The doors between the carriages also proved challenging because there were different types and varying methods of opening them. There was the push/pull type; the slide from one side type, which needed a lot of strength to open it; and the slide from the middle type. It was this one that foxed me for a bit in spite of the arrows pointing in opposite directions. I passed what must be a second-class compartment which was enclosed, with four seats either side, and made my way through two more third-class compartments which were full of a party who had travelled to the station by coach.

At the end of the carriage the window was open so it was possible to stick your head out and take photographs. The loo at the end of the carriage was out of order (so some things don't change, do they?), but I found another one further along the train which, to my relief, was working. The flush was interesting – there were two little pedals by the pan – one to press to fill it with water, the other to empty it. Very hygienic! I'm sure that would pass health and safety regulations. Hand-washing facilities with soap and towels were available, and the door could be locked by an old-fashioned simple sliding catch. (No slow revolving doors here!)

At last I neared the front of the train and the guard's van, where I chatted to the guard and asked, "Can I look in the first-class carriage, please? I am writing a book about trains." He was helpful and said, "If there is room on the way back, you can sit in first class so you can compare the experience of the two carriages." I explained that I was travelling with two friends. He paused for a moment, and then said they could join me in first class too.

"Wow! That's great. I didn't expect such VIP treatment. Thank you very much."

The first-class carriage really was a cut above the rest with individual blue spacious seats. These were free-standing armchairs with legs and expensive-looking upholstery. The tables had polished wood surfaces, as did the carriage walls. There were brass hooks at the end of the carriage for coats and wooden shelves for luggage.

There were individual little lights on the wall above the tables, each with its own pretty glass lampshade. It had a homely feel about it, rather like a lounge and was certainly more comfortable. It was lighter too than the other carriages because it was at the front of the train behind the engine so the end windows allowed more light in.

I made my way back through the train to find a very large bottle of Old Speckled Hen waiting for me. It's a long time since I have had a bottle of beer and I had forgotten that they are a litre. "I think I will be rather spaced out if we don't have lunch soon," I said to my sister.

The train wandered through the countryside and at one point the track looped back on itself to avoid a flooded area where the original line used to go. It's very strange because you can see the front of the train coming along the track in what appears to be the opposite direction to you as we go round the bend.

It was a pleasant enough journey through the Welsh countryside, and we stopped at a little station, typically painted in brown and cream, before continuing to our destination.

As we drew into Portmadoc it was possible to see different seabirds feeding in the estuary – oyster catchers and dippers. I wished I had binoculars with me but have taken some photographs which might show them clearly when downloaded on to the computer.

At Portmadoc we enjoyed a fish and chip lunch in the station café and had a little time to look around the station and view the engine.

The guard kept his word, and although there were now some people in the first-class compartment we were able to join them on the return journey to Ffestiniog. This time we treated ourselves to a Baileys, which I felt was more fitting to first-class passengers than an Old Speckled Hen!

We managed to find the route home without any difficulty.

It has been an excellent day out, I wish you could have been there to share the experience; maybe we can find another steam railway closer to home later in the year.

Love, M

LETTER 24.

1st March 2009

Dear B

The sun is shining and it promises to be a straightforward journey home with a fast train to Euston. M and D brought me to Stoke station to catch the 12.15, but as we went onto the platform, a train pulled in with Euston on the front, so of course I got on, saying a hasty "Goodbye" to M and D.

Once on the train, I turned to wave at them and my sister had her nose pressed against the window, trying to tell me something. I could just work out that she was saying, "This is a slow train." Oh well, never mind, I thought, it's too late to get off now. So I found a table and began to do some work. The guy opposite me was Chinese, and I asked him, "Do you know what time the train arrives in London?" He shook his head and replied, "Sorry, I don't know. I'm getting off at Nuneaton."

Fortunately, the train manager appeared in our compartment shortly afterwards to check the tickets. He was very helpful and informed me that this train will arrive into Euston at four o'clock! At that rate I might get home by midnight! I had checked earlier on the Internet to discover there were engineering works on the line, where I need to get off, and a bus service is operating between Brighton and Shoreham. I had rung home and BJ had agreed to collect me from Hassocks instead because that is quicker.

I asked the train manager, "Can I get to London by a faster route?" He consulted his timetable. "You can change trains at Stafford and catch a fast train to Euston, arriving at 2 p.m."

That sounded better. I might just make the connection via the underground to be on schedule again.

It proved an advantage to get off at Stafford because I just had time to buy a sandwich (chicken salad and no mayonnaise) before the Virgin Pendolino arrived on time. Pendolino sounds romantic as a name but it's just a type of train that can apparently safely 'lean' around curves up to 20 per cent and thus goes faster, giving you a gentle ride. I'm not sure about that. I sometimes feel a little nauseous as we round bends at speed.

I like the fact that trains have names; I suppose it's a romantic notion really. I remember First Great Western Railways in 2006 asked for suggestions from passengers for their favourite places along the various routes in the West Country and 50 were selected to be displayed on the side of the engine. What a splendid idea! Trains have also been named, I think, after famous people. John Betjeman, the poet, has a train named after him and it appropriately travels on the London to Norwich line, probably because it passes through Diss, about which he wrote a poem: 'A Mind's Journey to Diss'.

I remember the poem because it is addressed to 'Dear Mary', although I have no idea who she was!

It's so much more romantic to travel on a train with a name which means something, although I think 'Thomas' and other famous toy trains have not yet ended up on the real McCoy.

We took the children to Drusilla's zoo when they were over from New Zealand. They have a miniature train there painted like Thomas and, as you travel round the track, 'Gordon' and 'Percy' can be seen in the sidings. I don't think the engine driver would like to be called a 'Fat Controller' or even a thin one, for that matter. Anyway, it was fun, and the adults enjoyed it as much as the children!

The train was on time at Stafford and I easily found a window seat with a table and a point to plug in my laptop, so all is well again. I then needed to visit the loo which is always difficult on these trains – well, slightly embarrassing anyway because the door is remotely controlled by a push button and it takes forever to open. If there are lots of passengers they inevitably watch as you go in and press the close button which also seems to have a remarkably slow effect on the door. Then you have to remember to press the lock button, and it is a relief when it clicks and you now have some degree of privacy. There is always a niggle at the back of my mind, though, that maybe the door will remain shut and you will be trapped inside for a very long time and may have to press the emergency red button to be let out! There is a notice underneath telling you to wait for assistance!

The toilet was clean today and even had a purple plastic toilet cover and a picture of two little ducks above it. There was soap, water and a hand dryer and also a large mirror and pegs to hang things on. I think this might be useful if like me a passenger is in a rush and needs to put make-up on, comb hair, etc. en route.

I had to wend my way through two carriages to reach the loo, but this was quite easy without luggage because you can almost swing between the seats from one handhold to another. (Rather like our ancestors swinging through trees perhaps.) The only tricky bit was negotiating the legs sticking out or arms reading newspapers halfway across the aisle or passengers who suddenly decided to get up to reach overhead luggage. But I managed it and was relieved that my laptop and luggage were still where I left them. I guess it's unlikely that anyone will steal them on a train that doesn't stop for two hours. If anything was missing, I suppose I could alert the train manager who could search the train or even ring ahead for the transport police at Euston!

Today, sitting opposite me was a lady of Asian origin with a lot of luggage, she seemed to be very tired and kept putting her head down on her case. Across the aisle, three friends in their twenties, I think, were more vociferous and fidgety. They were all in white tops, blue denim jeans and trainers. Funny how if you were to ask youngsters to wear a uniform they usually object and yet kinda end up all looking the same anyway. One had a white flat cap, just to be a bit different, and had various bits of ironmongery in eyebrows, nose and ears. They returned from the shop with of course chocolate, crisps and fizzy drinks. Health education in schools and colleges, and adverts via the media really don't seem to have much effect, do they?

I checked the underground pocket map, which I always carry in my bag, and calculated that if I travelled on the Victoria line tube I would be able to get the connection because there are only a few stops on this route.

I groaned inwardly when the train was due to arrive ten minutes late into Euston, which is cutting it really fine to get across London. To save time, I went to collect my suitcase from the luggage rack at the end of the carriage only to find it was jammed in tightly beside another case. I tried to manoeuvre it and then with a bit more force and frustration tugged at it. To no avail, it was well and truly stuck!

Examining the situation more closely, I could see it was caught on the side-pocket zip (which was undone) of the pink case that's underneath it, so I gently tried to wiggle it free and just as I gave it a final yank, hoping that I had not damaged the pink case, the young guy who had been sitting opposite me offered to help. I politely declined his assistance, and with my rucksack on my back and suitcase in tow, I set off through the train with the intention of jumping out at the front and saving a few minutes' walking time. It was quite a trek to the front of the train and entailed walking through four first-class carriages. Fortunately there weren't many passengers in them today to glare at you as you invade their space. There were no staff to prevent this little time-saving ploy, I guess if lots of people did it there would be congestion getting off the train but today it's OK. Perhaps at weekends people are not commuting to and from work and are in less of a hurry.

I rushed across the station concourse and a tube drew in almost immediately. The train driver must have got my telepathic message to hurry up because we hurtled at great speed through the tunnels. The train was crowded which is unusual for the Victoria line but was probably because the Circle line was closed for engineering works this weekend; that must be so frustrating for folks, having to keep changing lines to get to their destination. It takes ages to walk from the platforms from one line to another, and sometimes it even means changing levels and using the escalator.

The situation was not helped today by a large pushchair blocking the doorway as I got on, but there's no point in complaining because I think the mum and her friend are speaking in French. Although I know a little and could complain with a few expletives, they probably would not be appropriate, and my accent and mispronunciation would make them laugh or think I'm really odd. Anyway, the baby was cute and responded to my game of Peep Bo. I was relieved when they left the tube before me at Green Park with lots of other people. The carriage was almost empty then, so maybe the passengers were going to stroll down the Mall or get a connecting train on the Jubilee line.

At Victoria there was the usual crush to go up the steps to the platforms for mainline trains, so that slowed me down a bit. At the top I tried to scrutinise the information boards as I arrived onto the concourse, wishing I had better long sight because I kept bumping into people in my haste to see the time and platform for my train to Brighton. The clock showed 2.30 p.m. and the train was due to leave from platform 18 at 2.32! Platform 18 is right across the other end of the station and there wasn't another train for ages.

It was time to really speed up! I scurried across the front of the station as fast I can, wishing I was wearing flatter shoes and weighed two stone lighter. I could see the train was still there and, fortunately, the barrier was open and I didn't have to waste precious seconds putting the ticket in the automatic barrier and waiting for it to come out again before I could reach the platform. The ticket checker waved me through as I held up my ticket and several other people like me were rushing for the train and the doors were closing! "Please wait," I shouted pleadingly. "Please wait!" and the guard with one foot in his door, which is always last to shut, held it open for me. Bless him!

I made it and collapsed, out of breath, panting like one of the proverbial steam engines, into the nearest seat.

I have one friend who sees catching the train at the last minute as a regular challenge. She has timed the journey from home to her local station to perfection and has on more than one occasion arrived as the train is about to leave and thrusts her umbrella between the doors to prevent them closing. Perhaps that's why there is now a minute delay after the doors have closed before the train departs.

What a relief when the service trolley appeared soon after we set off. Rarely has a Kit Kat and cup of railway coffee tasted so good!

Tearing off the chocolate wrapper, I managed to get chocolate all over my fingers because my hands were so hot, but I didn't care today. I licked each finger individually so as not to waste any and finally used the paper napkin which was wrapped round my coffee cup to complete the job.

I was sitting in a single seat in a narrow corridor outside the loo. Funny place to have a seat! I don't think it's meant for people to sit to wait if the engaged sign is up. Opposite was a seat and space for people who are in wheelchairs. What a horrible place for them, right outside the loo!

I think I should write to the railway company about it. It wouldn't be rocket science to design a space in the main compartment for wheelchair users with access. Where are any accompanying friends or carers supposed to sit?

Three or four people visited the loo on the journey, and I can empathise with them as the door slowly revolved at the push of a button on entry and exit. Been there! Done that! Know how it feels! There were various noises from inside, but I tried to ignore them and couldn't be bothered to look for another seat.

This train was driven by a guy in a hurry, and we sped through the outskirts of London and into the surrounding countryside. I rarely travel on Sundays and the train was obviously taking the scenic route and stopping at more stations.

Often the train divides at Haywards Heath and I hoped I was in the right part of the train. I asked the man opposite me but he didn't know and left the train at the next stop, Purley… Purley! Am I on the right train?! I listened out for the station announcement and it was OK, this really was the country route! The train manager too confirmed this immediately and after every subsequent tannoy announcement. I call it the parrot effect!

It's St David's Day but I didn't notice anyone wearing a daffodil. I think they are late this year after the cold snap at the beginning of the month; but when I left home on Wednesday the daffodils were in bud on the bank. The primroses were out in the garden and there was the usual carpet of snowdrops in the churchyard along the lane. Looking out of the window, there were signs of spring – the hazel trees full of catkins dancing in the breeze, and the silvery grey buds of fluffy pussy willow bursting through. I love springtime with the lighter nights imminent, and the summer months with warmer weather to come.

There is so much housing development everywhere; mainly small houses in terraces and modern blocks of flats. They remind me of the Lego houses I used to build with the children. I would hate to live in a flat or house without a garden.

When we passed Three Bridges and the train drew into Gatwick I relaxed, knowing that I was indeed on the right track.

BJ was waiting at Hassocks for me, and I was glad to be home and look forward to a day off tomorrow.

I am looking forward to you coming next weekend.

Love, M

PS. I have found John Betjeman's poem about Diss where he describes the countryside on the journey and his expectation of enjoyment with his travelling companion, Mary Wilson. It is written in rhyming couplets and describes their proposed meeting at Liverpool Street station, and whether or not to travel first class to avoid reporters. He then embarks on a vivid description of the countryside and his observations of the houses and churches along the route before their slow arrival into the isolated town of Diss.

M

Dear B

Weather! British weather! It must be the only country in the world where you can experience four seasons in one week.

The dilemma this morning was what to wear. It has been bright and sunny this week and I have completed lots of jobs in the garden, but today it is overcast and it has rained overnight and the black clouds overhead are threatening another downpour. Oh well, no worries, I thought. I put on a jacket and went out to the car to be hit by a biting east wind so returned to the house to put on another layer. I have left my waterproof coat at your house so I also had to take an umbrella, although I don't know if it will stay up if it does rain.

All was well as I drove to the station and bought my ticket except I tried to use my bus pass again by mistake! The ticket guy sighed inwardly and had a kinda long-suffering look on his face as he kindly asked me if I also have a senior railcard. I fumbled around in my purse and he helpfully reminded me that it's dark blue. Eventually I found it and for the first time purchased a day travel ticket which included the underground, since my Oyster card has no money on it. I hoped none of the automatic machines would eat my ticket because it's the only one issued today in place of the usual two – one for the outward and one for the return journey.

This reminded me of the first time I met BJ. It was at the station in Sevenoaks and I was on my way home to the West Country via London. I joined the queue at the ticket window and after a short while realised that the queue was not moving but getting longer behind me. At the front of this line of people was a woman arguing with the ticket seller about the type of ticket that could be exchanged for the voucher she had for a conference in London. The voucher was apparently for a return fare but he would only sell a single ticket, insisting that she acquire another voucher at the conference. This, pointed out the woman, was sharp practice since the return fare had been paid by the company. It was a hopeless argument, and a single ticket was finally issued as people in the queue became increasingly anxious about missing their trains. I vaguely recognised the argumentative person as a colleague at the school where I worked. Later she was to become a lifelong friend and companion. That's BJ, and I discovered the incident I had just witnessed was so out of character. Over 30 years later we are still close friends and share the same house, and rarely does BJ feel so strongly over an issue and protest so vehemently!

It was cold in the wind on the platform but there was not long to wait, and for once I was not buying coffee at the kiosk. The usual cheery girl is not there and so I gave it a miss.

SPLATT! Wow! A pigeon overhead just missed dumping on me. It's supposed to be good luck if the pigeon shit lands on you, but I'm glad it didn't! I mean, what would you do if it did score a hit? At best you'd have to get it cleaned off in the ladies' loo and miss the train. At worst, go home and change and arrive very late in London.

Today people were standing as they often do in a row, silent, unmoving, like a row of statues or maybe more like penguins at the zoo because everyone faced one way, looking for signs of the approaching train. As the train appeared the 'silent statues' moved forward as though conditioned and without a word proceeded to board the train.

I sat in a seat with a table for my laptop but the sun was in my eyes and I couldn't see a thing, so I hoped to change seats at Hove where usually lots of folks get off. Good. Today was no exception and I moved across the corridor. Hope the guy next to me wasn't offended or thought maybe he had BO, but I doubt he's even noticed because he's so absorbed in his book.

The train conductor was on the ball today or maybe he's just started at the front of the train and so appeared to check the tickets. Have you ever looked at them closely (the tickets, I mean), especially on the reverse side?

It says travel is subject to 'National Rail Conditions of Carriage (NRCoC). Copies can be obtained from the staff at any railway station or from national rail website.' I wonder if anyone has ever bothered to do this; maybe I will look them up one day or ask the staff for a copy, but I bet they are dead boring!

At Haywards Heath one poor lady (about my age) almost fell into the carriage, completely breathless. Poor soul, she must have really run to catch the train. I know the feeling, and there are no vacant seats. The age of chivalry is obviously past because none of the 'gentlemen' present offered her a seat. I would have let her have my seat but I was by the window and hemmed in by another guy fixated by his book. It's a commentary on Shakespeare's *Tempest*. I'm always interested in what other people are reading; sometimes you can guess their profession. Maybe he's a mature student.

This could be my last visit to London for a while, at least to work with students, and I'm just daydreaming and reflecting on some of our weekends in the capital.

Remember our visit to London last summer when the weather was warm and sunny? Do you remember visiting Chinatown and having a meal in one of the restaurants?

We had Dum Sing so that we could sample a range of dishes. You are so good at eating with chopsticks, and I am always determined to try so it takes me twice as long to finish a meal! We wandered through Chinatown and you introduced me to durian, which is on sale outside one shop in a large barrel with a lid. It smelt awful, and you said you didn't like the taste but it's apparently a delicacy in the Far East.

I later looked it up on the web and found a comment from a guy who has lived there and actually now likes the stuff. I will include a copy when I post this letter.

Do you remember we then took a boat along the Thames to St Katherine's Dock where you used to have a boat moored? It's right by Tower Bridge and the Tower of London which we didn't have time to visit then but is on our list for the future. I have looked up some information about it and attached it at the end; it's yet another amazing place in London with quite a history attached to it.

Anyway, at St Katherine's Dock is the Dickens Inn where we had a snack and a jug of Pimms, freshly made and quite delicious! After this liquid lunch we returned along the river and were delighted when Tower Bridge opened just after we passed through it. The commentary about the bridge is interesting, and I have since looked up some more information about it. I will attach it to this letter when I get home tonight.

On arrival at Victoria I decided to try the coffee at the hotel on the station recommended by H. Walking from the station concourse, I entered from a side entrance and walked along a narrow corridor and was then faced with a choice of three or four different lounges/bars that all seemed to serve coffee.

I walked along confidently and found Chez Gerard, a rather comfortable French bar, mainly for business people, I think, judging from the clientele. There was a complimentary newspaper to read, which confirms my suspicions because it's the *Financial Times*. I feel duty-bound to borrow a copy from the counter and read it avidly!

It's also waitress service here and I am addressed as 'Madame', which I guess you would expect from the name of the bar. The coffee was excellent and accompanied by a small wedge of French chocolate (Valrhona, no less). It's not so bitter in taste as most dark chocolate, and I'm sure it was beneficial for my health! Well, that's according to *The One Show* on TV last night; although Adrian Chiles was unimpressed by the sample offered to him on the programme. Maybe I should 'blog' this vital piece of information to him!

I had only a £20 note to pay the bill. The waitress (Danielle), who didn't sound at all French to me, looked perplexed and asked, "Have you a credit card? because I have no change in the till." "No problem," I replied and produced the desired bank card and paid the princely sum of £2.10. "Thank you very much. You have made my day!" Well, that's good. She must lead a very boring life! I thought, but said: "Please could you tell me where I can find the Ladies?" She pointed out of the door, "Third on the left, past the Internet room." I thanked her; but finding the Ladies was a different proposition and, in spite of Danielle's clear instructions, it took me several minutes to find it. Passing several doors ominously marked 'PRIVATE', I eventually found it and it was worth the search – it was free! And clean! With not only soap and hand towels but hand cream to use after washing your hands. It smelt of coconut but I'm sure it's very good for my skin.

The next problem was to find my way out of the hotel by the same route as I came in – onto the station concourse. I walked several times up and down the corridor and investigated the hotel lounge and another bar before coming to the conclusion that I'm not going to find it easily unless I ask the doorman or approach the concierge at his desk. I thought this might look a bit suspicious because I came in through the back door and was carrying a rucksack which could have contained anything, especially since the lead of my laptop was half sticking out the side.

There was no other alternative but to boldly walk out through the front entrance and down the steps, which I finally did and found myself around the corner from the station in Buckingham Palace Road. Well, at least I wasn't lost and was able to continue my journey to Gloucester Road without further incident!

It has been a successful visit because my final student here in London has completed her portfolio. I am now on the train on the way home.

Hope you have had a good day.

Love, M

PS. Here are the descriptions of durian, the Tower of London and Tower Bridge:

Durian

Durian is described by Tony Morton on the internet as having the texture of a cold cow pat and smelling like a poorly maintained public loo. He thinks the taste is worse but I wonder if he has ever tasted a cow pat! This was how the Asian fruit durian was first described to him, by western expats living in Singapore. Unsurprisingly he avoided it like the plague. Then he met some local connoisseurs, who hold this fruit in very high regard. They claimed, "The texture is like baked custard, while the smell and taste are simply indescribable but delicious." So of course he had to try it. Perhaps we should sample it when we are next in Town!

The Tower of London

Wow, this is another of the amazing historical places in London which we must visit soon. Over a thousand years of history, starting with William the Conqueror in 1078 and taking nearly 20 years to build. It was built as a residence for monarchs on the outskirts of London, as it was then, for security and stands on the corner of one of the old Roman walls. The original tower was the White Tower, which symbolised strength and power and was supposed to intimidate the people of the city who were not too happy, I guess, at being defeated by a Frenchman at the battle of Hastings and accepting him as king.

Subsequent monarchs changed and enlarged the palace as its role expanded. It has housed the Royal Mint, the Royal Observatory and the Public Records. Oh, and of course the Crown Jewels, which survived the attempt by one Colonel Blood to steal them in 1671. Apparently, having killed the jewel keeper, he crushed the state crown under his cloak while his son tried to saw the sceptre in half and a third member of the gang stuffed the orb down his breeches! They were discovered by the jewel keeper's son, who raised the alarm and they were arrested. For some reason Charles II later pardoned him and gave him a pension. How strange.

There was also a menagerie here. The King of Norway gave Henry III a polar bear, and it was kept on a long chain so that it could fish in the river. Centuries later (1811), the Hudson Bay Company gave a grizzly bear to George

III which was named Old Martin, and he ended his days at London Zoo after 25 years at the Tower. It must be difficult for monarchs to receive unusual gifts, impossible to send them back or refuse them, and they create some problems in housing them. Lions were part of the menagerie in1741 and were also given names: Marco and Phyllis plus a cub, Jenny.

The more gruesome use of the Tower as a prison and torture chamber, with many tales of execution, and villains being hung, drawn and quartered close by on the green, sends shivers down my spine, although I would like to visit it, and risk future nightmares and sleepless nights!

The Yeoman Warders, or beefeaters, guard the Tower and are servicemen with at least a 22-year service record. No one is quite sure about the origin of the nickname 'beefeaters', but it may have started with the fact that part of their salary was in cuts of beef or that they were invited to eat as much beef as possible from the King's table.

One of them is responsible for the care of the ravens. It's not clear when they became part of the Tower, but it is well documented that Charles II moved the Royal Observatory to Greenwich rather than move the ravens when the Royal Astronomer complained about them. The legend of the ravens is that if ever they leave the tower, the monarchy will crumble. To prevent these rather vicious birds from flying away, the Yeoman Ravenmaster hand rears them so that they are tame, feeding them on a daily ration of beef from Smithfield Market. One of the wings is clipped to prevent them flying away, but they are free to roam the grounds.

There have been many famous and notorious inmates at the Tower. Guy Fawkes among them as well as many monarchs who fell out of favour, notably Anne Boleyn and Catherine Howard, the unfortunate wives of Henry VIII accused of adultery and treason. Elizabeth I also was imprisoned here by her half-sister Mary who suspected Elizabeth of plotting against her.

There is so much to explore and learn about the history of the country here. We must go soon to find out more and perhaps try some of the things on offer, like trying on a gauntlet, lifting a musket and waving a sword! (Hope that's not just for kids!) It's also possible to buy Tic Tac Toe, which is a sort of noughts and crosses game but a bit more complicated with many variations.

I once dressed up as a beefeater for an advertising event with our local historic house, St Mary's in Bramber. It was a strange costume and the ruff around my neck was very itchy. I liked the buckled shoes, but was not too keen on the tabard and stockings. The crowning glory was indeed the wonderful hat!

Tower Bridge

Tower Bridge, unlike the Tower of London, is only just over a hundred years old. It was built in 1876 because the population of London had increased so much and London was still a busy port. A competition was launched by the City of London Corporation to design a new bridge across the Thames. Inevitably, a committee was set up to discuss the issue and judge the designs. The problem was twofold: how to provide a bridge without disrupting the passage of the many ships along the river, and secondly, a means for vehicles and pedestrians to cross. What a challenge for Victorian architects!

The city architect at the time, Horace Jones, came up with the idea of the double bridge and his design won the competition and work began on the bridge. Unfortunately, he died before its completion and the work was supervised by an engineer, John Wolfe Barry.

An act of parliament was passed to ensure that the specifications and safety were adhered to and that disruption to the river traffic would be minimal. It took eight years to complete and involved eight contractors with responsibility for different aspects of its construction, and the employment of over 400 workers to build it. Eleven thousand tons of steel were used in its construction, and this was protected by the addition of Portland stone and Cornish granite. These two materials were intended to give it a more pleasing appearance, but on completion many Londoners apparently thought it rather hideous! Perhaps we get used to new landmarks over time. I think it's quite spectacular and the views from the top across London are amazing. The colour of the bridge has changed. Originally it was chocolate brown but was repainted in red, white and blue for the Queen's Silver Jubilee in 1977.

It's called a 'bascule' bridge, which is the French word for see-saw. The two bascules are operated by a hydraulic system which is now powered by oil and electricity. Originally steam was the source of power, produced in huge boilers and stored in accumulators. It only takes a couple of minutes to open and close the bridge, as we saw on our boat trip. I wonder what happens if there's a power cut.

Unusual events have happened during its history; in 1952 a No. 78 double-decker bus was crossing when the bridge began to open and the driver had the presence of mind to accelerate rather than get stuck on one of the bascules at an awkward angle and crash. He successfully bridged the three-foot gap without any serious injuries to all on board.

A pilot, Lt Alan Pollock, flew a Hunter Hawk jet fighter under the bridge to celebrate 50 years of the RAF and as a protest because the senior officers were not going to mark the occasion with a fly past. The poor man was arrested and discharged from the forces on medical grounds. Perhaps any stunt involving risk not only requires a measure of courage but also a little insanity!

President Clinton on a dinner date with Prime Minister Tony Blair returned in his motorcade across Tower Bridge and the bascules began to rise to let through *Gladys*, a Thames sailing barge, splitting the party in two, much to the consternation of the security. Apparently the American Embassy didn't answer the telephone call to warn of the opening of the bridge. Time and tide waits for no man, as the old adage says!

Two further incidents amused me. In 1999 a man drove two sheep across the bridge to exercise his right as a Freeman of the City of London and to demonstrate how the rights of people are being eroded. This right dates back to the thirteenth century and allows people to drive cattle and sheep across the bridges in London. And people apparently do this from time to time.

In 2003 a man dressed as Spider-Man climbed the bridge to campaign for the organisation Fathers 4 Justice. He managed to stay there for six days, resulting in the closure of the bridge and the inevitable congestion in the city.

Tower Bridge has undergone renovations this year so I think we really must explore it soon, but I think we won't try any stunts to become famous, unless you have any ideas...

LETTER 26.

4th April 2009

Dear B

I have been thinking that it's time we had another weekend in the capital now that spring is here.

There are a number of good offers for hotels in the paper and I have been checking out what's on at the theatres.

We enjoyed *Billy Elliott* at the Victoria Palace last time, but I think we will stay in a different hotel. It was just about OK but the Hilton at Paddington was better; perhaps we could go back there. I'll check out a range of deals, and then we can get our diaries together to see when we are both free.

We have seen *Mary Poppins* and *Blood Brothers*; I've seen *Wicked*, the *Phantom of the Opera*, and recently you saw a production of *Joseph* in Southampton.

You took the family to see the *Lion King* and I haven't yet, but I think BJ would enjoy that too. There are several ballets coming up and the old classics like the *Mousetrap* and *The Woman in Black* are still going strong.

We could see *Mama Mia* again but maybe *Oliver* with Rowan Atkinson would be a good choice.

We could also take a boat along the river again and lunch at the Dickens Inn. I would like to visit the Houses of Parliament this year and the Old Bailey, but the Tower of London is right by St Katherine's Dock so that's another real possibility.

The only disappointing place for us was Madame Tussauds, which was very crowded, where we had to queue for ages to buy tickets and it was impossible to get near any of the wax figures.

We could go to a gallery or another museum; we did enjoy Tate Modern and the Science Museum last year. Retail therapy along Oxford Street or King's Road might be the place to find some real bargains, or even a return visit to Harrods in this time of credit crunch.

Helen has been telling me about some other visits to London, and possible places to have lunch. They vary from Langan's to the Blueprint Café and Gordon's Wine Bar, among many others. Recently she met up with friends at an interesting place, the Watermen's Hall, the home of the Company of Watermen and Lightermen of the River Thames. Apparently Watermen look after people, and Lightermen barges (a lighter is a barge that carries cargo).

The first hall (mentioned initially in 1603) was completely destroyed by the Great Fire of London. It was rebuilt on the same site, but moved to its present site, just off Lower Thames Street, in1780 to a new building designed by William Blackburn.

Perhaps this is a place we could visit for lunch; it sounds fascinating, and it's not far from Waterloo. We could also book a tour there to see the beautiful eighteenth-century architecture.

Any ideas? There's so much to see and do in the capital. I will leave it up to you to decide.

Perhaps we can make a decision when we next meet.

Love, M

REFERENCES

Betjeman, John, *Collected Poems* (Murray, 1980).

Lear, Edward, *The Complete Nonsense of Edward Lear*, ed.
   Holbrook Jackson (Faber and Faber, 1975).

www.daveys.co.uk   Information about the Crusting Pipe.

www.en.wikipedia.org   Information about Grosvenor Square.
                                    Information about St Paul's Cathedral.
                                    Information about the Great Exhibition.

www.harrods.com   History.

www.hrp.org.uk   Information about the Tower of London
                                        and other royal palaces.

www.news.bbc.co.uk   Information on naming trains.
                                    Opening of the Diana Memorial Fountain
                                        by Her Majesty The Queen.

www.royalalberthall.com   History of the Royal Albert Hall.

www.royalparks.co.uk   Information on Hyde Park.

www.themangotree.org   Information about the restaurant.

www.websingnet.com.sg   Morton, Tony – information on durian.

www.westminster-abbey.org   Information about Westminster Abbey.

Royal Albert Hall photograph by Ted Rosen
http://www.sxc.hu/photo/232483

Grosvenor Square
http://en.wikipedia.org/wiki/File:Grosvenor_Square.JPG

Hyde Park photograph by Agata Urbaniak
http://www.sxc.hu/photo/951035

Tower of London photograph by Agata Urbaniak
http://www.sxc.hu/browse.phtml?f=download&id=952843

Tower Bridge photograph by Agata Urbaniak
http://www.sxc.hu/browse.phtml?f=download&id=952844

About the Author

Mary Christine Levett was born in Somerset to working class parents just after the Second World War. Educated at Bishop Fox's School Taunton, she subsequently trained as a science teacher at Homerton College Cambridge and embarked on a teaching career working with all ages. In the mid 1980's Mary decided on a change of career and trained to be a nurse achieving RN status; both professions where a sense of humour is essential.

Returning to the field of education as a lecturer in Health and Social Care, she currently works as a care assessor for NVQ with a local company (Elizabeth Training). The visits to London described in *Capital Letters* emanated from this work and she developed a greater interest in London. These inevitably triggered off memories of past visits and experiences of travel. Her enthusiasm for writing stems from journal writing and the preparation of educational materials for all ages.

The influence of West Country culture with its characters and intrinsic humour formed the basis for looking at life in a light hearted way. As a science teacher observation was essential for both people (pupils in particular) and the natural world. These two influences have been brought together in her debut book *Capital Letters*.